THE BISHOP OF LIPOPPO

A FABLE

BY

GERALD T. McLAUGHLIN

12/1/2009

Christine & Jerry

Enjoy !

Jerry McL.

iUniverse, Inc.
New York   Bloomington

The Bishop of Lipoppo
A Fable

iUniverse books may be ordered through booksellers or by contacting:

iUniverse
1663 Liberty Drive
Bloomington, IN 47403
www.iuniverse.com
1-800-Authors (1-800-288-4677)

Because of the dynamic nature of the Internet, any Web addresses or links contained in this book may have changed since publication and may no longer be valid. The views expressed in this work are solely those of the author and do not necessarily reflect the views of the publisher, and the publisher hereby disclaims any responsibility for them.

ISBN: 978-1-4401-3465-4 (pbk)
ISBN: 978-1-4401-3466-1 (ebk)

Printed in the United States of America

iUniverse rev. date: 5/20/2009

THE BISHOP OF LIPOPPO

A FABLE

Dedication

On June 2, 2003, the twenty-fourth anniversary of our marriage, my wife, Irene, wrote me a letter about the years we had spent together. "At the top of our list of wonderful things," she wrote, "we have been blessed with two outstanding boys, each of whom is wonderful in his own special way. We feel that God has made us stewards of great gifts in these boys. We have also been blessed with countless friends, many of them true, true friends who have come forward to help us in our hours of need. Maybe it's at the bottom of the list of wonderfuls, but we are great hosts and our many dinner parties have always been splendid only to be outdone by more splendid Christmas mornings with champagne and wrapping paper flowing abundantly."

Irene died five months after these words were written. I dedicate this book to her and to our sons, Mark and Matthew, for whom we acted as God's stewards. I also dedicate the book to my daughter, Helen, who has started on her stewardship with the birth of her son, Viggo.

Reviews

The Bishop of Lipoppo is an uproariously funny and witty fable, which resonates with Thurberesque insights into the modern condition.
—Barry Hawk, attorney, Skadden, Arps, New York

I have edited many books and would have to say that *The Bishop of Lipoppo* is one of the funniest, wittiest, and most touching books I have ever worked on. I loved it!
—Terrie Barna, editor, Pacific Palisades, California

Little did the black African priest, Father Harbinger, know when he stepped on the plane to Rome that he was beginning a spiritual journey. His story will enchant you as you participate in his adventures with the Bronx Zoo, the UN, Harvard University, and the Catholic Church.
—Deacon Dwight Morton, Equestrian Order of the Knights of the Holy Sepulchre of Jerusalem, Diocese of Phoenix

Contents

Chapter One
Father Harbinger Goes to Rome

"I really took a spill, didn't I, Banda?" Samuel Harbinger, parish priest of the remote Kenyan village of Lipoppo, held onto Banda's mane as he pulled himself up off the ground. A short black man with sparkling eyes and a contagious smile, the thirty-nine-year-old Harbinger steadied himself before taking his first step.

"I must have gone over the handlebars of the bicycle. I was lucky I landed in the grass."

The lion growled sympathetically.

"But answer me this, Banda .Why did that lioness attack me? I was riding my bike, and minding my own business. You must know why."

Banda growled again, this time as if he got his paw caught in a cookie jar.

"Don't try to change the subject, Banda. I know all your tricks."

Suddenly, Harbinger's eyes opened wide. "Oh, I bet I know why your furry friend attacked me. She's jealous of our relationship, isn't she?"

Banda growled a third time. "Three growls! I'll take that to be a yes."

Harbinger dusted off his cassock and stood his bicycle up against a tree.

"Do me a favor, Banda. Explain to her the nature of our relationship. You were three days old when I found you lying dehydrated at the edge of the water hole. I took you to the rectory and with Mobeki, the village mechanic, we taught you how to lick food off a spoon and sip water from a cup. You and I have been friends ever since."

Harbinger paused for a moment. "Banda, while we are on the subject of relationships, let me raise a related issue. I think you know what it is. Lately the Council of Elders has been hearing complaints from some of the villagers. You've been coming into Lipoppo looking for food. Some villagers have come home and found you in their kitchens eating their dinners."

Banda paced back and forth, flicking his tail as if swatting flies but saying nothing.

"Remember when you were three months old, Banda, you stepped on hot coals and burned your front paws? You came down with a high fever. No one knew what to do, not even the old shaman who lived on the outskirts of Lipoppo. Finally, the whole village contributed money to pay for a trip to Nairobi to see an animal doctor. I had to carry you into the doctor's waiting room in a basket."

Banda rolled on the ground and held up his front paws.

"Yes, I know they are completely healed, but that's not why I brought up the incident.

I want to remind you that the trip to see the doctor in Nairobi was paid for by the villagers. Without their help, you may have died from infection."

Getting up off the ground, Banda resumed his pacing.

"You are no longer the frisky cub you once were. You are a full grown lion and quite an intimidating one at that."

For a moment, Banda looked puzzled.

"Oh, I'm sorry. Intimidating means threatening. Sometimes I forget that you are still only a lion. The elders asked me to talk to you. You can't come into the village like you used to. People are afraid of you. The elders want you and the rest of your pride to stay east of the line of acacia trees. The trees have always been the border between Lipoppo and the savannah."

Banda continued to walk about angrily, this time his tail seemed to be swatting tennis balls.

"Banda, stop storming about in a huff. Sit down and concentrate on what I am saying to you." Harbinger took a chocolate bar out of his pocket. "I shouldn't be doing this, but if bribery is the only way I can get your attention, then I guess I'll have to use bribery."

When he saw the candy bar, Banda sat down and started to smack his lips. His eyes lit up with anticipation.

"Okay, take the chocolate bar, but listen carefully to what I'm saying. You must obey the Council of Elders.and stay east of the acacia trees. If you don't, you run the risk of a villager taking a shot at you. That mane of yours would bring a handsome price on the black market. I love you too much to see that happen. Now off with you. It's almost midnight, and I still have to prepare my sermon for Mass tomorrow. Sundays are supposed to be days of rest but not for parish priests."

Banda playfully tried to put his mouth in Harbinger's pocket.

"You've gotten your bribe. You're not going to wheedle another piece of chocolate out of me. You know what happens when you eat too much candy, it rots your teeth, and then we have to take you to a dentist. You can imagine how big a production that is."

Harbinger started to wheel his bicycle toward Lipoppo. He stopped a moment. "Remember, Banda, do what the elders want. Stay to the east of the tree line."

As Harbinger passed the water hole and came to the outskirts of the village, a cold rain began to fall. Shivering, he pulled his cassock tight around him. When he reached the rectory, he saw

3

that his housekeeper Bagua had thankfully left dinner on the kitchen table. After he finished eating, Harbinger took out a pencil and pad and outlined his sermon for tomorrow's Mass. He would call his homily, "On the Fifth Day God Created the Animals."

* * * * * *

Early the next morning, Father Samuel Harbinger awakened to a loud knock on the door of the rectory.

"Wake up, Father. We must show you something. It's important."

The priest recognized the voice of Obani, the postman. Harbinger opened the door and was surprised to see the whole village gathered in front of the rectory.

"Why are you all up so early? Mass doesn't start for another two hours."

"It's because of the letter, Father Samuel."

"What letter, Obani?"

"The one that arrived yesterday. The Council of Elders says it's from the pope."

"From the pope?"

"Yes."

"Give me the letter, Obani."

The postman took it out of his pocket and handed it to Harbinger

The priest took a knife and slit open the envelope.

"The elders were right, it is from the pope."

"What does it say, Father Harbinger? We couldn't read the words."

Father Harbinger looked askance at the postman.

"Obani, has someone already opened this letter? Remember, Jesus taught us to tell the truth."

Obani began to stammer. "Father Samuel, yes I opened the letter, but it was already half open."

"Half open?"

"Well, maybe it was not half open, but it was at least a little open."

"Obani, how may times have I told you not to open other people's mail … particularly mine? A priest receives confidential things in the post."

"The Council of Elders got so excited when the letter came that they wouldn't wait until you came home. They voted to have me open the letter."

"Well, Obani, you are the postman of Lipoppo. You cannot allow letters to be opened by strangers … no matter what the Council of Elders says."

"It will not happen again, Father."

"Good. Now let me read what the pope says."

Obani stood looking over Father Harbinger's shoulder. "The letter is written in a strange language."

Harbinger smiled. "This strange language is Latin."

Father Harbinger scribbled a note on a piece of paper. "When Mass is over, Obani, drive to the village of Woomba and give this note to Father Albert. I need his help. He was always better at translating Latin than I was."

* * * * * *

Father Harbinger had hardly given the final blessing ending Mass, when Obani bolted out of church and jumped into the village Jeep. Blaring his horn, the postman went barreling down the road toward Woomba, in the process overturning Imbala's vegetable stand.

A thunder squall had blown in from the south as Obani reached Woomba. The clatter of raindrops on the roof of the Jeep was almost deafening. When the wind finally blew the storm away, Obani ran up the steps of the rectory. He pounded excitedly on the front door.

"Who's there?" a cranky voice spoke from inside the building.

"I'm Obani, the postman from Lipoppo. I'm looking for Father Albert. I have a message for him."

"Come back later. Father's not here now."

"Are you his housekeeper?"

"Yes. Yobate is my name."

"Well, Yobate, the message I'm bringing is special delivery."

"Special delivery?"

"Yes."

Obani knew the effect the words "special delivery" would have on Yobate. To a housekeeper, a special delivery item must be treated as if it were sent by God himself. It must be given top priority. Everything else should be put on hold until the delivery is made.

"He's in church saying his prayers. Father Albert doesn't like to be disturbed. He'll only make an exception for Lacata."

"Who is Lacata?"

"A woman Father Albert is counseling. Her husband and son were killed in a car accident a year ago. I told Father that she grieves too long, but he always answers, 'Yobate, wounds heal faster for some than for others.'"

* * * * * *

When Father Albert read Harbinger's message, he left the church and hurried back to the rectory.

"Yobate, I must leave for Lipoppo as soon as possible. Cancel my eight o'clock meeting tonight with Lacata."

The housekeeper smirked. "The woman will be angry that you are canceling a meeting with her."

"She will understand when I explain the reasons why. Father Samuel needs my help in translating a letter from the pope. It's in Latin. By the way, have you seen my Latin dictionary?"

"Yes, Father Albert. It's on top of your nightstand. It has been there since last year."

"Really?"

Yobate threw up her hands in comic frustration. "Yes, Father Albert, really!"

* * * * * *

Father Harbinger greeted his friend and fellow priest at the front door of the church.

"Albert, thanks for coming so quickly."

"I understand you have some Latin to be translated—a letter from the pope no less?"

"Yes, but before we begin, Albert, remind me again about Latin conjugations and declensions. You decline verbs and you conjugate nouns, right?"

"No, it's the other way around."

"I don't think I'll ever get that straight."

"Well, what about *ibi* and *ubi*? In the seminary, you always mixed them up."

"*Ibi* means there and *ubi* where."

"Good, Samuel. Last test, *filius,* and *filia.*"

"*Filius* is daughter and *filia* is son."

"No. *Filius* is son and *filia* is daughter."

Father Harbinger threw his arms up in exasperation. "Mixing up *filius* and *filia* can be embarrassing. Thank God you're here, Albert."

"And thank God I found my old Latin dictionary from seminary days. We'll need it to translate words accurately."

After working on the letter for several hours, Father Albert looked up from the table.

"I think I know what the letter says, Samuel."

"Well, tell me."

"Hold your breath, my fellow pastor. It says you are being

ordained a bishop in Rome on January sixth, the Feast of the Epiphany."

"Albert, translate the letter again. You must have overlooked something."

"I haven't overlooked anything, Samuel. You have been selected a bishop. That's what it says."

"But why was I chosen?"

"Maybe because you are deserving of the office. Let me tell the villagers the good news. They'll be so proud of you."

Father Albert walked outside and stood on the top step of the church.

"His Holiness Pope Linus II has selected your pastor, Father Samuel Harbinger, to be made a bishop. He will be ordained in Rome on January sixth, the Feast of the Epiphany. That's just, four days from now."

The announcement set off a wave of dancing in the streets of Lipoppo. People weren't exactly sure what a bishop did, but whatever it was, they were glad that their parish priest would now be able to do it.

* * * * * *

As one might expect, Samuel Harbinger was thunderstruck. No one from Lipoppo had ever been made a bishop before. Why was he chosen to be the first?

Father Harbinger hurried to the village phone and dialed his older brother Vincent in New York City.

After what seemed an eternity, Vincent picked up the phone.

"Vincent, this is your brother Samuel. How is your club doing?"

"Fabulously, bro. But you didn't call all the way from Lipoppo to ask about the club."

"You're right. I need a favor."

"What kind of favor?"

"Well, the pope has invited me to St. Peter's in Rome to be ordained a bishop."

"Ordained a bishop! In St. Peter's ! Are you sure?"

"Yes. Father Albert translated the letter, and he's sure he made no mistakes."

"Well, little bro, I'm proud of you. But you said you wanted to ask me a favor?"

"You remember how our parents taught us to bring a gift when we were invited to someone's home?"

"Yes. It's a way of thanking the person for his generosity."

"Well, I would like to bring a gift to the pope—to thank him for the promotion. But I have no idea what to get him. Mother always said you were the best problem-solver in the village. Could you help me, Vincent?"

"Of course, I'll help you. Tell me this. Does the pope have any hobbies like collecting stamps, coins, or antique clocks? If he's not a collector, maybe he plays golf and you can give him some clubs."

"Father Albert read somewhere that the pope likes music."

"Rock, jazz, blue grass, opera, or classical?"

"Unfortunately, Albert didn't finish reading the story."

"Let me see what I can do."

"There's one more thing, Vincent. The gift has to get to St. Peter's in Rome by January sixth."

"That's four days from now. You don't give me much time, do you?"

"I'm sorry, but the invitation just came today."

"Don't worry, Samuel. A gift will be at St. Peter's by January sixth."

"What will you get?"

"Whatever I get will surprise you and the pope."

"Before you hang up, Vincent, can I ask you a personal question? You are the only family member I have left."

"Go ahead. This sounds serious."

"I'm not sure that I should go to Rome and be ordained a bishop."

"Why not?"

"I barely graduated from the seminary and my sermons show it. They are simple stories about animals and the people of Africa. I'm afraid that the hierarchy in Rome will find them childish, maybe even silly. They will expect me to give homilies on fine points of theology and dogma, not on a crippled boy named Gabriel and his elephants."

"Samuel, don't belittle your sermons. They teach the people of Lipoppo about God in ways they can understand. Jesus did the same with his parables. Remember, he spoke about the shepherd and his flock, not about transubstantiation. As for grades, since when does a transcript measure the worth of a person? If it did, I would be out of work. I never went to school a day in my life."

"And what about my stutter and the stool I have to use to be seen over the podium?"

"Now you are really beginning to sound silly, younger brother. Would Jesus' message have been any less profound if he had to stand on a pile of stones to deliver it? Would Jesus' message have been any less meaningful if he had been born dumb and others had to preach it for him? Stutters and stools have nothing to do with how good a priest you are."

"And I can't drive a car. I must ride my bicycle everywhere I go."

"Bicycles are popular in Rome. You can get around the city pretty well on them. By the way, Samuel, I forgot to tell you. I can't drive, either."

"Vincent, I know you are right, but no matter how hard I try, the doubts keep coming back."

"Whenever you face change, Samuel, there are worries and misgivings. It is only natural. But if you decide not to go to Rome, I'll come and take you there myself, at gunpoint if necessary. Promise me you'll go."

"I promise. But don't you forget to send a gift to St. Peter's.."

* * * * * *

That night, Father Harbinger called the villagers of Lipoppo together.

"My friends, I must leave you for a while."

"Father Albert says you are going to Rome, Father Samuel." There was concern in Obani's voice.

"Yes, I must go to Rome to be made a bishop."

"Why must you be made a bishop?" It was Zamba, the village blacksmith, who asked the question.

"The pope wishes it. He is the head of the Catholic Church. I must obey him."

Zamba shook his head. "We believe in Jesus because of you, Father Samuel, not because of the pope. We do not care whether you are a bishop or not. All we care about is that you stay our parish priest—that you baptize our children, marry our sons and daughters, and bury our dead."

Hestern, the village carpenter, nodded in agreement. "Yes, Zamba is right, Father Samuel. We don't care whether you are a bishop. If the pope insists on making you one, let him come here to Lipoppo to do what has to be done."

"The pope appoints bishops in cities and towns all over the world. He cannot travel to all these places and still govern the Catholic Church. I must go to him."

Hestern asked another question.

"If there is room in the Jeep, can some of us go with you?"

"Hestern, Rome is far away from Lipoppo. To get there, you would have to take an airplane from Nairobi. I'm afraid I must go by myself."

Then Obani voiced the concern that was on every villager's mind. "I am told that people in Rome are dangerous drivers. They drive their cars and bicycles on the wrong side of the road. Please, Father Samuel, be careful when you ride your bicycle. Look both ways and do not ride at night."

Father Harbinger could barely hold back his tears. He loved

these villagers all so much. Although it was presumptuous on his part, Samuel had prayed to God for a favor. If God were of a mind to deny any villager from Lipoppo entry into heaven, Samuel asked if he could speak on that person's behalf. Since God had never asked him to come to the defense of any villager, he assumed that everyone who died in Lipoppo had been admitted into heaven.

"I will return as soon as possible. While I'm gone, Father Albert has promised to help in emergencies. Catechism classes, however, will have to be canceled. In their place, I ask each one of you to help at the AIDS clinic. Write down all that you do. If you can't write, then ask Obani to help you. When I come back, I wish to read what each and every one of you has done. We must build a new clinic, and I will need all your help."

* * * * * *

Early the next morning, the townspeople tied Father Harbinger's bicycle to the roof of the village Jeep and escorted their parish priest to the outskirts of Lipoppo. They all knelt on the ground while he blessed them. Then with Nelson, the owner of the local bank, driving the Jeep, Father Harbinger began his journey to the Nairobi Airport seven hundred kilometers away.

As they drove past the water hole, Banda ran out in front of the Jeep. Nelson slammed on the brakes barely missing him.

"Father Samuel, can't you teach Banda to be a bit more cautious in flagging down the village Jeep?"

"I'll do my best, Nelson, but as much as I hate to admit it, Banda is only a lion. He doesn't fully understand lots of things. Remember, God created the animals on the fifth day, not on the sixth day like us."

Father Harbinger got out of the Jeep and walked over to Banda. Purring loudly, the lion put his paws on the priest's shoulders. In return, Harbinger gave Banda a friendly tug on his mane.

Suddenly, a lioness herding several cubs came out of the

shadows and loped to where Banda and Harbinger were standing. A moment later, a second lioness with a cub dangling from her mouth joined the group. After a chorus of growls, grunts, and roars, all the lions got down on their haunches. Harbinger made the sign of the cross over each one of them, leaving Banda for last. When he was finished, he hung a small wood cross around Banda's neck and returned to the Jeep.

"What was that all about, Father?"

"It was a good talk. Although he was a bit miffed, Banda has promised to stay east of the acacia trees."

"And the cross?"

"Banda asked me for one. I wouldn't expect any imminent conversion, however. He tries to be like me, that's all. Let's go, Nelson. We have a long ride ahead of us."

At the Nairobi Airport, Nelson took Father Harbinger's piece of luggage out of the backseat of the Jeep. "I see you have a black bag like almost everyone else in the world. Take my advice, Father. Put some picture or identifying mark on your suitcase. Otherwise, when you get to Rome, it'll be a nightmare trying to find your luggage."

Choking back tears, Father Harbinger embraced Nelson and said good-bye. With his bicycle and luggage in tow, he entered the terminal and checked the list of departing flights for the next plane to Rome. Egypt Air Flight 850 to Cairo with connecting service to Rome was scheduled to leave Nairobi in five hours. Harbinger bought a ticket, but before checking his luggage through to Rome, he thumbed through a discarded magazine and found a picture of a sleeping hippopotamus. With some tape borrowed from an Egypt Air representative, he pasted the picture on the side of his black bag. He then bought a bottle of Coca-Cola, took out a book about Francis of Assisi, and settled in to wait for the plane to Cairo.

* * * * * *

13

On the flight between Cairo and Rome, Father Harbinger sat next to a portly man with big, bushy eyebrows and an arched nose. The man's rumpled suit and blue polka dot bowtie gave him a distinctly, professorial look.

"Introductions are in order. The name's Bonti, Sergio Bonti. I'm a reporter for Rome's daily *Il Messaggero*. I've been on assignment in the Middle East for several weeks, mostly in Damascus and Jerusalem."

"Nice to meet you. I'm Father Samuel Harbinger, a Catholic priest."

"Where do you work, Father?"

"In a small village in Kenya called Lipoppo. It's about a six-hour drive northwest of Nairobi."

"Why are you flying to Rome?"

Just then, an Egypt Air flight attendant came along the aisle taking dinner orders.

"Mr. Bonti, I see you have ordered a kosher meal."

"Yes."

" Father Harbinger, will you have chicken or pasta for your main course.?"

"Pasta. I am a vegetarian."

"Thank you." The flight attendant continued down the aisle taking dinner orders from the passengers..

Harbinger was curious."Tell me, Mr. Bonti, what is a kosher meal? We do not have this type of meal in Lipoppo."

Bonti laughed. "That's because you don't have Jews in your village."

"Do you need Jewish people to have a kosher meal?"

"Usually they go together. Kosher means that the food has been prepared according to Jewish dietary laws."

"So my housekeeper, Bagua, could make either kosher hippo stew or non-kosher hippo stew?"

"I didn't know there was such a thing as hippo stew, but if there is, I guess it could be made kosher or non-kosher. But, Father Harbinger, you never told me why you were going to Rome."

"Pope Linus II is going to make me a bishop."

"You seem young for the job. I thought you had to be thirty-five years old to be ordained a bishop."

"I'm thirty-nine. I hope I am on time for the consecration ceremony. My letter arrived in Lipoppo only two days ago. The pope must be a good man to reach out to someone like me. My village of Lipoppo is so small. It is not on many maps."

"That's not the case with the Vatican. It may be small, but it's on everyone's map. Never underestimate the power and influence of the pope."

"Yes, Signor Bonti, you are right. He is the Supreme Pontiff of the Roman Catholic Church, Vicar of Jesus Christ on earth, Sovereign of the Vatican City State, Bishop of Rome and Servant of the Servants of God."

"Quite frankly, Father, I don't give much credence to this last title. To me, the pope is a world leader and an international power broker. He is not anybody's servant. What I find fascinating as a non-Catholic is to see how the pope exerts his influence on world affairs."

"What do you mean?"

"There are roughly thirty-five hundred bishops throughout the world. The pope meets with each of them periodically, usually once every five years. These meetings are important. They constitute a dialogue between the pope and his bishops over the state of the church. They also allow the pope to exercise influence on governments through his bishops."

"But, Signor Bonti, how does the pope find the time to have these meetings? If he meets every bishop once every five years, that would mean meeting roughly two bishops a day. On top of that, of course, is his regularly scheduled list of private and public audiences. With so many people to meet and so much to do, how does the pope find time for prayer and meditation?"

"He probably doesn't."

"I must speak to the Holy Father about his own spiritual life.

Unless he finds the time to talk to God, how can he guide the church?"

"Good question, Father Harbinger. Maybe the job of pope has become too demanding for one man. But the present pope is probably the last person on earth who would ever admit that."

"Why?"

"Pope Linus was born Benat Detchepure. The name says a lot."

"What do you mean?"

"He's a Basque, and Basques are a fiercely proud people. I doubt that a Basque pope would ever admit that the job was too big for one man. His pride will never admit that."

"I didn't know that about Pope Linus. Well, I'll try to cheer the Holy Father up a bit. I'm bringing a gift to thank him for inviting me to St. Peter's to be ordained a bishop."

"What are you giving him?" Bonti leaned back. Obvious curiosity crossed his face.

"I don't know, exactly. My brother Vincent knows all about gifts. He has promised to deliver a present to the pope by January sixth. He wants it to be a surprise both for me and for Pope Linus."

As the two men talked, Bonti was struck by the simplicity and openness of this parish priest from Lipoppo.

"Father Harbinger, with your permission, I would like to do a story in *Il Messaggero* about your becoming a bishop and the gift you're bringing to the pope."

Harbinger's eyes lit up with excitement. "Would there be pictures?"

"Yes, of course."

"And will you send copies of the newspaper story to Lipoppo?"

"Yes. How many do you want?"

"Would you send five? I will pay for them."

"Five? I think the paper can do better than that. If you let me do the story, I'll have our circulation department send fifty copies to your village. There will be no charge."

Father Harbinger smiled. "Then you can do the story."

"Good." Bonti took a business card out of his wallet.

"Here's my number at *Il Messaggero*. Give me your business card so we can stay in touch."

"I do not have a business card."

Bonti smiled. "Oh that's right. Priests like to refer to them as 'name cards'. When the Gospels are your stock and trade, I guess 'name card' sounds better than 'business card.'"

"I'm afraid I have neither, Mr. Bonti."

"Well, I would recommend buying some sort of card as soon as you get settled in Rome."

"Do priests in Rome actually have these cards?"

"A better way to phrase the question would be: does any priest in Rome not have one?"

* * * * * *

As the Egypt Air flight from Cairo prepared to land at Rome's Leonardo da Vinci Airport, Sergio Bonti pointed out the window to the dome of St. Peter's Basilica looming over the city.

"No matter how many times I see it, I'm awestruck by the size and grandeur of St. Peter's. Someone once called it a place like no other. That's true even for a Jew like me. You'll see the effect the basilica has on you when you've been in Rome for a few days."

"But you have been in Jerusalem. You must have seen the Church of the Holy Sepulcher—the place where Jesus was crucified and rose from the dead."

"Yes, but it doesn't compare to St. Peter's."

"Well, someday I hope I will be able to go to Jerusalem and see the holy places for myself. It is one of my two goals in life."

"I'm sure you will. Just remember not to be too disappointed." Signor Bonti paused a moment. "You said going to Jerusalem was one of your two goals in life. Would you be offended if I asked you what your other goal is?"

"No. It is to be the best priest I can for the people of Lipoppo."

* * * * * *

Father Harbinger's heart pounded with excitement as the wheels of the plane touched down on the runway. As the plane taxied up to the gate, Harbinger could not help wondering why all this was happening to him. He was, of course, grateful for his promotion. As a bishop, he would no longer have to squabble with the Nairobi Archdiocese over the scheduling of confirmations. Harbinger could perform the sacrament himself whenever it was convenient for the children and their families. But Harbinger couldn't believe that smoothing administrative tensions was the reason for his appointment as a bishop. There had to be something else, something deeper and more fundamental to the life of the church than confirmation schedules. Harbinger would have to wait and see what God had in store for him.

Gathering his few belongings from the plane's overhead compartment, Harbinger said good-bye to his traveling companion, Sergio Bonti. As he left the plane, Harbinger scribbled two reminders on a scrap of paper: buy calling cards and check on the pope's gift.

Father Harbinger went to the baggage carousel to find his suitcase. Nelson was right, of course. People were pushing and shoving, trying to find their black bag. Thankfully, Harbinger had no difficulty in finding his. While there were many black bags, there was only one with a picture of a sleeping hippo taped to its side. After he retrieved his bag, he went in search of his bicycle. A security officer directed Harbinger to the airport information desk.

"Start there and never give up hope."

Barely visible amid piles of schedules and maps, a uniformed official stood at the information desk gamely answering questions.

"What are you looking for, Father?"

"A bicycle."

"What flight was the bicycle on?"

"Egypt Air Flight 850."

"Did you actually see the bike loaded on Flight 850?"

"No, but ..."

"Well then, it could have been put on another Egypt Air flight, possibly in Nairobi or in Cairo."

"I guess so."

"Under the circumstances, I really can't help you. You'll have to deal directly with Egypt Air. Persevere and you'll find your computer."

"I'm looking for a bicycle, not a computer."

"Well, don't forget to tell them that. Good luck with Egypt Air."

* * * * * *

Two long hours later, Harbinger found his bicycle in a SAS duty-free shop. How it got there was a mystery to all. As he wheeled his bicycle out of the terminal, a car with Vatican license plates pulled up alongside him. A young priest with gold-rimmed glasses and a mane of flaming red hair jumped out of the car. His ruddy complexion and round face gave him a distinct boyish look, so much so that some might have thought him too young to hear confessions.

"Father Ignatius Cropsy here. Are you Samuel Harbinger, the episcopal candidate from Lipoppo?"

"Yes."

"Thank God, I've found you. You're the last candidate to arrive."

"Getting my bicycle took much longer than expected."

"Ah, you must have been caught up in the intricacies of Italian baggage handling. Just remember when something can't be found, it's always someone else's fault."

Father Harbinger smiled. "Am I too late for the day's events?"

"The walking tour of the Vatican has already started, but if we hurry, we can get you checked in at the Domus Sanctae Marthae in time for this evening's panel discussion."

"What's the panel discussion about, Father Crotsky?"

"Cropsy's the name. The discussion is called, Dioceses for Beginners. It will give you inexperienced 'baby bishops' a chance to hear how senior bishops run their dioceses. And as a bonus, you'll get a chance to meet my boss, Cardinal Martin Jensen, prefect of the Congregation for Bishops. He'll moderate the session."

"I've never met a cardinal before."

"Well you are about to meet one of the most powerful in the church. Jensen is a workaholic. He had a bout with colon cancer two years ago but emerged from it looking younger than before. He is seventy-one years old but he looks like a main in his sixties. And when you get a chance, listen to his voice. It thunders like the voice of an Old Testament prophet just returned from Mount Sinai."

"Is Jensen a possible successor to Popr Linus?"

"Yes, but he wouldn't be my choice."

"Why not?"

"He's a conservative like Pope Linus. We've had too many conservative popes. We need someone who will lead the church in a new direction."

"While we are on the subject of Pope Linus, tell me one thing."

"What?"

"Why did the Holy Father take Linus, the name of the second pope, to mark his pontificate?"

"There's only one person who can answer that and that's the pope himself. All he said at the time was that he wanted to rescue one of his predecessors from obscurity. Some of us hoped there was more to it than that."

"What do you mean?"

"He's a Basque and Basques are outsiders. We hoped the choice of name was a signal that the new pope wanted to return the church to a more autonomous, less authoritarian structure—a structure that had existed during the first century when Linus was pope. Our hopes got another boost when he announced that he would hear confessions on Good Friday."

"Like an ordinary priest?"

"Yes. But despite Pope Linus' choice of name and willingness to go into the confessional, the Basque in him did not come out. He has not adopted a more flexible attitude with respect to most issues. On anything significant, he follows in the footsteps of his predecessors. The only things that really seem to interest him are abstruse canon law issues."

"Like what?"

"Like whether a proper genuflection requires the knee to touch the ground, or whether a Catholic can satisfy his Sunday Mass obligation by attending a service conducted by a schismatic priest—that sort of stuff."

"Perhaps the pope is simply cautious by nature. Being pope is an awesome responsibility."

"Whether a pope refuses to move, is afraid to move, or moves too slowly, the result is usually the same. Nothing of significance happens. I'll give the pope high grades for one thing; however, he's courageous. He carries a bullet lodged in his chest to prove that."

"What do you mean?"

"When he was Archbishop of Bilbao in Spain, a group of Basque terrorists stormed city hall and captured the mayor and several members of the city council. Without giving advance warning to either side, the archbishop walked unaccompanied into city hall and returned a day later with an agreement ending the takeover."

"How did he get shot?"

"Someone tried to assassinate him a week later. Whoever tried almost succeeded."

"And the bullet is still in his chest?"

"Yes, doctors say it is too dangerous to remove." Cropsy looked at his watch. "Let's get going. We can talk more about the pope later."

"Just one more question."

"It's getting late, but go ahead ask it."

"Tell me what will be discussed at the question and answer session."

"I imagine issues like disciplining clergy, empty pews, dealing with the media, and untangling disputes with 'central command.'"

"Central command? I don't understand."

"I mean untangling disputes with the Vatican."

"Disputes over what?" asked Father Harbinger.

"Over things like the age of confirmation, the power of bishops' conferences, and diocesan finances.'"

"I will have no dispute with the Vatican over finances. My parish has little money. Whatever there is, I keep in a desk drawer in the rectory."

"Where do you keep your own money?"

Father Harbinger smiled. "It is rare that I have money of my own. A month ago, Hestern insisted that I take money for baptizing one of his children. 'Buy some new shirts the next time you are in Nairobi,' he told me. 'The ones you have are getting threadbare.'"

"Did you buy the shirts?"

"Yes, but I put whatever was left in the desk drawer. Are there other issues which might cause friction with the Vatican?"

"What about disciplining priests? You must have heard of the recent scandals involving the clergy."

"I will also have no problem with the Vatican over that."

"It is a problem for every bishop I've ever met."

"I'm the only priest in Lipoppo. I have no one to discipline but myself."

"What about media relations?"

"Again, I will have no problem with the Vatican over these relations."

"Why not?"

"In my village, there are two computers, one phone line, and one fax machine. Zamba, the blacksmith's wife, uses the phone too much. She's always calling her daughter in South Africa to see how her grandchild is doing. Sometimes she calls four or five times a day. Every now and then, I have to remind her that if she keeps using the phone so much, she'll have to install her own line. Other than with Zamba's wife, there are no problems."

"You must be experiencing low attendance at Mass?"

"No. Attendance at Mass has never been higher."

"You must have some problem to contend with?"

"Well, there is one."

"What is it? I promise I won't tell."

"Recently, I have tried to increase the number of children coming to Mass. I let them bring their pets to church."

"I assume these pets you are referring to are wild animals?"

"Yes, but to be allowed into church, the wild animal must be tame."

"Who determines that?"

"I do. I have turned down a water buffalo and a hyena, but I have said yes to a cheetah cub and several monkeys."

"Amazing! Has your policy increased the number of children at Mass?"

"Yes. Attendance has doubled."

"Well then, what's your problem?"

"I don't know if it's really a problem—it's more like an issue."

"Problem—issue? Tell me what it is."

"Well, a chimpanzee ran off with a parishioner's shawl. The woman expects the church to pay for it. I refused. Do you think the church is liable, Father Crispy?"

"It's Cropsy. Ask your question at the Q and A session. If nothing else, I'm sure it will enliven debate."

"What happens after the session?"

"Sorry, I forgot to give you this schedule of events planned for the next two days."

Cropsy handed Harbinger a wrinkled piece of paper labeled, Episcopal Ordination.

"As you can see, the next two days are very busy—the recitation of the rosary later tonight, various lectures tomorrow morning, a reception with the mayor of Rome in the afternoon, and a prayer vigil at night. The day after tomorrow, of course, is the ordination."

"Is there a tour of Rome on the schedule?"

"No, but if you would like, I'll give you the personalized Father Ignatius Cropsy church-by-church tour of Rome."

"Is it all churches?"

"Well, I could add in a few fountains and maybe the Coliseum."

"Could you also add in the zoo?"

"The zoo?"

"Yes, I've never seen a tiger before."

"Okay, we'll stop at the Rome Zoo. It's actually not called a zoo anymore. It's a Biopark. The Eternal City is doing a little up scaling."

"Where and when shall we meet, Father Causeby?"

"Cropsy! How about after the ordination ceremony? I'll meet you at the front entrance to St. Peter's."

"Okay. I'll be there, Father ..."

"Cropsy."

"I always have difficulty with Welsh names."

"Actually, the name's Scottish. I'm Glaswegian."

"Really?"

Harbinger had no notion of what a Glaswegian was but was too embarrassed to ask. "How many Glaswegians are there in Scotland?"

"Just over six hundred thousand. We can discuss Glaswegians some other time. We don't want you to be late. Throw your bike into the boot and get into the car. Mr. Manelli is sitting in the back."

"Who's Mr. Manelli?"

"He's the head Vatican tailor. You didn't send back your measurements. On your way to the Vatican, Manelli will have to outfit you as best he can. Whatever he says goes. He is the ultimate authority on anything having to do with ecclesiastical dress. This year, fifty-two episcopal candidates chose to come to Rome for their ordination. Manelli and his colleagues are having a busy time of it. Finishing up fifty-two new cassocks, miters, and crosiers is a big job."

"Seminary was a long time ago. Is the crosier the bishop's staff or is it his conical hat?"

"The crosier's his staff; the miter's his conical hat. Here's another one for you. What's a bishop's fascia?"

"I don't know. Is it his cape?"

"No, it's his sash. You have a lot to learn, my soon-to-be-bishop of Lipoppo. Just out of curiosity, why did you choose to fly all the way to Rome to be ordained? It's a bit of a trip. The letter said you could have been ordained in your local diocese in Africa."

"I don't remember getting the letter about choosing to be ordained either in Rome or in Lipoppo. When was it sent?"

"Months ago. I guess God wanted you ordained here in Rome. By the way, you still haven't put your bicycle in the car."

"It won't fit, Father Ignatius. We'll need some rope to tie it on the roof."

"There's no rope to be had. Just leave the bike here with an Egypt Air representative, and I'll get it later."

"The bicycle was a gift from my parents. I won't leave the airport without it."

"You're an obstinate one, Harbinger, but I guess that's why they made you a bishop. Get in the car. I haven't been on one of these contraptions in twenty years, but I'll get it back to the Domus where you are staying."

"Thank you, Father Ignatius. Could I ask you big favor?"

"Of course! What is it?"

"Before I leave Rome, I would like to say Mass in St. Peter's."

"There are over forty altars in the basilica. I'm sure I can find you one to use. Now off with you."

Led by a police escort, the car with the Vatican plates sped out of Leonardo da Vinci Airport. Father Ignatius Cropsy, his red hair blowing in the wind, wobbled his way behind on Samuel Harbinger's bicycle.

* * * * * *

Flanked by four of his episcopal colleagues, Cardinal Martin Jensen opened the question and answer session at precisely 7:30 PM. Cropsy was right, thought Harbinger. Jensen's voice did sound like that of an Old Testament prophet.

Samuel Harbinger listened intently to the back and forth between the panelists and the newly appointed bishops—"baby bishops," as Father Cropsy called them. As his Glaswegian friend had predicted, the majority of the questions focused on finances, disciplining priests, and media relations. Just as the session was about to end, Father Harbinger raised his hand.

"I see we have one more question." Jensen nodded to Harbinger. "Please state your name and diocese."

"Father Samuel Harbinger from the diocese of Lipoppo in Kenya."

"Unusual name you have, Father Harbinger. Go ahead with your question. I would ask you to be brief—our time is almost up."

"Thank you, Your Eminence. In my village, some children won't go anywhere without their pets, even to church. So to increase the number of children attending Mass, I started allowing boys and girls over seven years of age to bring their pets to Sunday Mass."

"You did what?" A look of incredulity passed over Jensen's face.

"I started allowing children over seven to bring their pets to Sunday Mass. The number of children coming to church has doubled. But then a chimpanzee ran off with a parishioner's shawl. The woman thinks the church should pay for a new one because it was stolen by a pet I let attend Mass. What do the panel members think?"

By now, the look on the cardinal's face had turned from incredulity to horror.

"Bishop Harbinger, whether they are pets or not, animals have no place at Mass. They disrupt services. Your policy must be stopped."

"But, Eminence, in Kenya, animals play a central role in the culture. Children treat their pets like family members. It is hard for someone from outside the culture to understand the closeness of the relationship. Let me try to explain using my own special relationship with Banda."

"Who is Banda?"

Harbinger laughed. "I just take for granted that everyone knows Banda. He's a male lion."

"You have a special relationship with a grown lion?"

"Yes. Lately he's been causing some problems in Lipoppo. So just the other day, I had to have a heart-to-heart talk with him."

"You had a heart-to-heart talk with a grown lion?"

"Yes, Banda has taken up coming into Lipoppo looking for food. The villagers complained to the Council of Elders."

Cardinal Jensen stood and stuffed papers into his leather case.

"You'll have to excuse me, Bishop Harbinger. I have more important issues to deal with than this. In the meantime, stop letting animals into Mass. The Vatican must study the sanitary, legal, and liturgical implications of what you're doing. Under some circumstances, your actions may be a venial sin."

As he left the room, Jensen muttered to one of his colleagues on the panel. "How did this priest ever become a bishop?"

"That's your area, Eminence. But I'll say one thing. If this priest is the harbinger of what awaits the church in the future, we are in for an interesting ride."

"Yes. Imagine a bishop of the church cavorting with a lion."

"Eminence, didn't Saint Francis cavort with the wolf of Gubbio?"

Cardinal Jensen gave his fellow bishop a cold stare. "I guess he did."

* * * * * *

Although upset by Cardinal Jensen's public scolding, Samuel Harbinger went to the recitation of the rosary in the Sistine Chapel—a venue chosen by Pope Linus himself.

As Samuel Harbinger filed into the chapel with his fellow episcopal candidates, he was overwhelmed by the blaze of color that greeted him. The ceiling panels depicted the Creation of Adam and Eve, the Fall and the Expulsion from Paradise, the Flood and the Sacrifice of Noah—a veritable painted Bible, as Harbinger later described it to Cropsy. Harbinger stared in awe at the fresco of the Last Judgment on the front wall of the chapel. Harbinger wondered how God could have given this man Michelangelo so much talent.

After Cardinal Jensen led the episcopal candidates in the recitation of the rosary, he said a few words about the history of the chapel and then took questions. Harbinger raised his hand.

"I see Father Harbinger has a question." Dislike and sarcasm dripped from every syllable the cardinal spoke. "I'm sure you want to know why Michelangelo did not paint a ceiling panel depicting the creation of the birds of the air and the beasts of the earth."

"No, that was not my question, Your Eminence."

"Then I apologize. Ask your question."

"Why are there no black faces like mine in these paintings?" Harbinger pointed to the Last Judgment. "Did Michelangelo believe that black people will not be judged on the last day like white people?"

Jensen looked annoyed. "Sixteenth century Italy was not a place where someone like a Michelangelo would encounter many blacks. Therefore blacks, and for that matter, Asians or Aborigines, are not included in his paintings. It's as simple as that."

Cardinal Jensen stood to leave. "It is difficult to see the panels on the ceiling unless you lie down on your back and look up. There are several pairs of binoculars on the altar for anyone who wants a detailed look at the frescoes. The chapel will be kept open during the night for those who wish to spend time looking at the ceiling panels."

As he left the chapel, Jensen noticed that Harbinger was lying down on his back and looking up at the ceiling. Jensen mumbled to himself, "He's probably still searching for a black face somewhere among the frescoes."

* * * * * *

A phone message from Sergio Bonti awaited Father Harbinger when he returned to his room. The message said that a camera crew from *Il Messaggero* would be at the ordination ceremony to take pictures.

Harbinger had just fallen asleep, when there was a knock at his door.

"Who is it?" The wall clock read 10:54 PM.

"Father, my name is Giovanni. I work downstairs at the switchboard."

Harbinger got out of bed, threw on a bathrobe, and opened the door. A tall, black-haired youth stood in the corridor.

"I'm sorry to bother you, Father, but a message was just

hand delivered for you from a Father Ignatius Cropsy. Normally, messages aren't brought upstairs after ten PM, but Father Cropsy asked if an exception could be made in this case. He thought you would like to get this message right away."

Giovanni took an envelope out of his pocket and handed it to Father Harbinger.

"I'm sorry, Giovanni. I can't understand Father Cropsy's handwriting. Can you read me the message?"

"Of course. Your friend says that earlier today he went to reserve an altar for you to say Mass in St. Peter's. While he was there, someone canceled next Tuesday's eleven AM slot to say Mass in the Clementine Chapel. Cropsy says he put a temporary hold on the slot. He is calling to confirm that the time's good for you."

"I think it is."

"Good. Then call and tell Cropsy it's okay. It's an honor to say Mass at the Clementine."

"Why?"

"The Clementine is the altar closest to the Tomb of St. Peter. Most priests think it is a great privilege to say Mass there."

Harbinger picked up the phone and dialed Cropsy's number. When no one answered, he left a three-word reply on Cropsy's answering machine. "Yes for Clementine."

"Thank you for taking the trouble to bring me the message. When do you work at the switchboard?"

"I work two shifts—from ten PM to six AM and from six AM to twelve noon."

"How old are you?"

"I'll be twenty years old next month."

"Do you go to school?"

"No."

"Why not?"

"I must earn money to support my brother and sisters. Someday I'll be able to go to school, but not now."

"Where are your parents?"

Giovanni looked away for a moment. "My mother died two years ago, and my father ran off with a streetwalker. I've had to keep my brother and sisters together as a family."

"How old are they?"

"I have a sixteen-year-old brother and two sisters—one fourteen and one eight. I try to keep the four of us together as a family."

Harbinger sensed that Giovanni wanted to say something more but was holding back.

"Is there something else, Giovanni?"

"Yes, my fourteen-year-old sister has AIDS. Many people avoid us. My brother wants to put her out and let her fend for herself. But family is family and I will not do it."

Tears started to fall down Giovanni's cheeks. "Aren't I right about that, Father? Family is family."

"Yes, family is always family." Harbinger thought of his brother Vincent.

"Thank you, Father. One feels so isolated in making these decisions."

"Doesn't the government or the church provide you with any help?"

"A few euros a month, but not enough to feed and clothe my brother and sisters."

Giovanni looked at his watch. "I have to go. Signor Duo will wonder where I went. He is always lecturing me on being on time."

"Who is this Signor Duo?"

"Cesare Duo is the director of Vatican telecommunications. Everyone who works in the Vatican knows him."

"Were you ever an altar boy, Giovanni?"

"Yes ... a long time ago."

"Would you like to serve Mass for me at the Clementine next Tuesday morning?"

"I can't. Signor Duo would not give me the time off."

"Suppose I asked Signor Duo to let you serve."

"He will say no."

"Even to serve Mass?"

"Yes. He'd say if I wished to serve Mass, I should do it on my own time. Thanks for the offer."

When Giovanni left the room, Harbinger knelt by the side of the bed and said a prayer for the young man. As he knelt there on the floor, he thought back to his own childhood, to the many happy times spent with his own mother and father and brother Vincent. He hoped that one day he and his brother would be able to share their feelings about that night. Mobeki had seen the accident. The Nairobi Road was muddy, he said. Samuel's parents were holding hands when the truck skidded into them. Mobeki said they both died instantly. Harbinger had always thanked God that his parents didn't suffer. After the accident, Vincent and Samuel went to live with their grandparents. When he turned sixteen, Vincent left for New York City. He never returned to Lipoppo. Yes, family is family, thought Harbinger, but sometimes the pain of remembrance is too great.

Chapter Two
The Dome of St. Peter's

When Cardinal Jensen awoke the next morning, he showered and hurried to his office at the Congregation for Bishops. "Get me Mabibin and fast." Jensen barked to his secretary.

Five minutes later, Majorcan-born Father Andre Mabibin entered Jensen's office. Pale and gaunt with carbon black eyes and long bony fingers, Mabibin had worked at the congregation for thirty years. "There's a certain ruthless quality about Mabibin," Jensen would confide to colleagues. "In his cosmology, there is heaven and hell but no purgatory. You are either right or wrong with no middle ground in between. You have to fear and respect Mabibin at the same time."

"You asked to see me, Eminence?"

"Yes, Mabibin. I want you to check on one of our episcopal candidates."

"Which one?"

"Samuel Harbinger. He's from some obscure village in Kenya. I think it's called Lipoppo."

"Yes, he was the last to arrive yesterday. Cropsy picked him up at the airport."

Mabibin's voice had a lifeless sound, as if his years of service in the Curia had drained him of emotions.

"How did this Harbinger become a bishop? Look at the nuncio's report on him and any other documents in his dossier."

"Yes, Eminence. Unfortunately, most of the dossiers have already been taken to the files. It may take a couple of days."

"Do it as soon as possible, Mabibin. And one thing more."

"Yes, Cardinal Jensen."

"You are a canon lawyer, aren't you?"

Mabibin nodded. "And a civil lawyer as well."

"I have a second assignment for you, Mabibin. Research whether a diocese is liable for items stolen in church by a wild animal allowed onto church property by the pastor."

"You say the pastor allowed the wild animal onto church property?"

"Yes."

"I will do the research, Cardinal Jensen."

* * * * * *

At precisely 10:00 AM the next morning, a fanfare of trumpets announced the arrival of Pope Linus II at the entrance to St. Peter's Basilica. A tall, acetic-looking man with gray black eyes and sallow complexion, the seventy-four-year-old pontiff had come to St. Peter's this rainy January morning to preside over the age-old Rite of Episcopal Ordination. Soon after his election to the throne of St. Peter, the new pope had expressed his views on the importance of bishops—middle management as he called them—in an impromptu interview with a reporter from *L'Osservatore Romano*, the Vatican's daily newspaper.

"An organization," he told the reporter, "needs both a good CEO and good middle management to be effective. The pope is the church's CEO and the bishops are its middle management.

The Holy Spirit selects the pope but the pope selects the bishops. To underscore the importance of appointing bishops, I invite all those appointed to the episcopate during the prior calendar year to come to Rome on January six, the Feast of the Epiphany, for their formal investiture as bishop. It is my way of recognizing their pivotal position in the structure of the church."

Pope Linus felt particularly gratified at the number of this year's acceptances—fifty-two, up from thirty-five the year before.

As the trumpet fanfare ended, Bishop Vergilio Patti, papal master of liturgical ceremonies, began the solemn march down the center aisle of the basilica followed by the fifty-two candidates. The papal choir thundered out the prayer to the Holy Spirit. "*Veni Creator Spiritus*, Come, Holy Ghost, Creator Blest."

When the candidates had processed down the length of the nave, it became the pope's turn. Although he had been pontiff for ten years, Pope Linus was a remote figure for most Catholics. His stern, humorless look earned him the name *il Papa Triste*—the Somber Pope. One seasoned Vatican hand, who had witnessed more of these papal liturgies than he cared to remember, wrote in his diary for that day, "Pope Linus must learn to loosen up. A little warmth goes a long way."

As Pope Linus approached the transept of the cathedral, the procession came to an abrupt halt. The pontiff signaled his personal secretary, Monsignor Paolo Remigi, to walk ahead and see what was causing the delay.

Trained as a diplomat at the Vatican's elite Pontifical Ecclesiastical Academy, the forty-year-old Remigi was seen as a rising star in the Vatican firmament. Pope Linus had recognized Monsignor Remigi's talents early on and appointed the trim and elegant Monsignor as his personal secretary. In that capacity, Remigi served as the Holy Father's troubleshooter, gatekeeper, enforcer, scheduler, counselor, and advisor. Because of his wide-ranging responsibilities and day and night access to the pope, church insiders came to regard Remigi as de facto the number two man in the Vatican.

Several minutes later, Remigi walked back to where the pope was standing.

"Well, what's the problem, Remigi?" There was impatience in Pope Linus' voice.

"Nothing unexpected, Holy Father. There's a camera crew from *Il Messaggero* taking shots of one of the candidates. People got out of line and it caused a mix up."

"Who is having his picture taken?"

"His name is Samuel Harbinger. He's the Bishop of Lipoppo."

"Where in God's name is Lipoppo?"

"It's a remote village in northwest Kenya."

"Kenya?"

"Yes. The poor bishop was mortified at the commotion caused by the camera crew. He says he'll apologize to you personally when he gives you the present."

"What present?"

"From what I can figure out, the bishop plans on giving you a 'thank you' present for inviting him to St. Peter's and ordaining him a bishop. His brother in New York was supposed to deliver the gift to the basilica by today. Then …"

"Then what?"

"Then, the bishop asked me if you had dinner plans for tonight. His housekeeper had sent some hippo stew with him and he wondered whether you would like to taste it—unless, of course, you are a vegetarian."

"Why in God's name would I ever want to taste hippopotamus stew?"

"He assumed that because you are the pope, you might like to taste the food Catholics eat in his village of Lipoppo."

"God has given me responsibility for the souls of Catholics, not for their stomachs. But this dinner invitation raises a bigger issue. Assimilating Catholics from the Third World into what is essentially a First World belief system may be the greatest challenge facing the church today. We will just have to grit our teeth and keep at it."

"Holy Father, why do you assume we'll be the ones doing the assimilating? To the Roman Empire, Christianity was the Third World belief system. Look what happened there. Maybe hippo stew will win out over pasta."

Pope Linus stood thoughtfully a moment. "What did you say the name of this Kenyan bishop is?"

"Harbinger, Samuel Harbinger."

The procession started up again.

* * * * * *

When he reached the high altar, Pope Linus genuflected, then turned and blessed the new bishops, their families, and invited guests. Today, the pontiff chose to give his blessing in Latin. As the pope's detractors were wont to point out, Pope Linus was "language poor"—at least by prior papal standards. Past popes had routinely been able to impart their blessing in twenty languages or more. Although he was fluent in five languages: Spanish, Italian, English, Latin, and Basque, two of them—Latin and Basque—were not widely spoken. As for Pope Linus' fluency in English, many pointed out that the word "fluency" should be kept in quotation marks. While the pope's vocabulary was strong, his pronunciation was heavily accented so much so that some audiences could not understand him. The confusion over Paolo Remigi's seminar is a case in point. Pope Linus announced that his personal secretary was going to Yale for a seminar. The audience thought he said Remigi was going to jail for the seminar.

Pope Linus took his seat on the papal throne and nodded to the Master of Ceremonies, Bishop Patti, to begin the liturgy. As the choir chanted the "Litany of the Saints," Bishop Patti walked over to where the candidates sat. One by one, the bishops stood up and stepped out onto the altar. As a sign of obedience to the Holy Father, each bishop would lie face down on the ground over the tomb of the first pope, Peter the Fisherman, and in front of his successor, Linus II.

A young Dutch bishop in line just in front of Harbinger pushed an aluminum walker. When it came his turn to prostrate himself on the floor of the altar, the bishop hesitated.

Harbinger gave the man an encouraging smile. "Go ahead. You can do it."

"The arthritis is so painful. I don't know whether I'll be able to get up off the floor."

"If you trust in God, everything becomes possible."

Leaning on the walker, the bishop let himself down to the floor. Then with Harbinger's help, he let go of the walker and slowly stretched out on the altar. Those in the church started to cheer and applaud when they saw what was happening.

"Now I must get up."

Harbinger held out his hand to the young bishop.

"Just hold onto me. Then slowly pull yourself up. Remember, Jesus got up off the ground three times even though he carried a cross. Think of him."

And the young bishop did think of him. And he pulled himself up.

* * * * * *

When the ritual of prostration was over, each candidate in his turn walked across the altar to a line of prelates led by Cardinal Ugo Carpaccio, dean of the College of Cardinals. As the candidates knelt one next to the other, the cardinals and bishops participating in the liturgy walked down the line pressing their hands on the head of each newly consecrated bishop. Hands on head, hands on head, this ceremony had persisted unchanged for two thousand years, creating an unbroken line of succession from the Apostle Peter down to the newest bishop.

When the ritual of the laying on of hands was over, the pope sat a moment listening to the "Litany of the Saints."

"*Sancte Luca, Sancte Marce.*" The choir chanted the Latin name of a saint.

The congregation responded, "*Ora pro nobis.*" (Pray for us.)

As the pope listened to the "Litany of the Saints," his mind wandered back to the first time he had ever heard it. When Benat Detchepure was eight years old, his mother had taken him to an Easter Vigil in the basilica of Our Lady of Begoña in Bilbao. The sound of the organ, the voices of the choir, the smell of the incense, the color of the stained glass, all merged into one glorious prayer to God. Benat grasped his mother's hand. To the eight-year-old boy, the experience was overwhelming. It was at this Easter Vigil that the future pope decided to become a priest.

Monsignor Remigi bent down and whispered in Pope Linus' ear. "Holy Father, the newly ordained bishops are waiting for you to invest them with the symbols of their episcopal office."

The Holy Father sat still for a minute more.

"Paolo, have Bishop Patti bring each bishop up to me. I will give each of them their crosier, miter, and ring."

* * * * * *

When it was his turn to approach the Holy Father, Samuel Harbinger followed the master of ceremonies to the papal throne. Harbinger looked around to see if a gift had arrived. If Vincent were planning a surprise, now was the time to present it to Pope Linus.

When Harbinger knelt before the pope, the pontiff embraced him and then handed him his ring, staff, and miter.

"Thank you, Your Holiness. I brought you something for making me a bishop. I'm embarrassed to say that I don't know what it is. My brother Vincent promised he would deliver it directly to St. Peter's."

Suddenly, as if responding to a cue, a Dixieland band accompanied by a small chorus of singers materialized from inside the church. Clapping their hands rhythmically, the singers vocalized "When the Saints Go Marching In." Then a young priest on the altar started to clap his hands and sway to the rhythm. A second priest joined in, then a third. Although he stoutly denied it, even the staid dean of the College of Cardinals, seventy-nine-year-old Cardinal Ugo Carpaccio, moved his hips to the sound of the music. The audience cheered in delight. Samuel Harbinger pulled a stunned Pope Linus up off his throne.

"In Africa, when a man's heart is full, he dances. Come, let us dance together, Holy Father."

A horrified pope looked at Bishop Harbinger. "A pope does not dance. It is undignified and would scandalize many in the church."

"Why, Holy Father?"

"Dancing has sexual overtones. It is the work of the devil."

"But not always. Try it, just this once. Dancing is good for the spirit."

Despite his objection, Harbinger swirled the pope around in circles. Struggling to break free from Harbinger's grasp, Pope Linus knocked his gold miter off his head. It flew across the altar landing in the lap of a startled episcopal candidate from Austria.

Harbinger's joyful dance with a not-so-pleased Pope Linus caused the Swiss Guards to go on red alert. Their first and only priority is the safety of the Holy Father. Several guards in their plumed helmets and striped uniforms dashed up the steps of the altar and wrested Pope Linus from Harbinger's rhythmic dancing. Then, with clock-like precision, other guards closed all basilica doors and emergency exits. As more and more members of the corps arrived, they fanned out through the basilica collaring musicians and marching them into the sacristy. For the most part, the chorus members were cooperative except for one rather overweight baritone. He would not stop singing and had to be poked with a Swiss Guard's ornamental halberd before he would agree to move into the sacristy.

* * * * * *

A harassed Paolo Remigi bounded up the stars of the papal throne. The panel of his Blackberry was producing sounds and colors he had never seen or heard before.

"Holy Father, order the Swiss Guards to reopen the doors of the basilica immediately. There are wild rumors circulating through Rome about the closure."

"What rumors?"

"A friend of mine called to see if five terrorists were holding you at knifepoint and demanding eight million euros in ransom. I had hardly squelched that rumor when another friend called. 'Was it true, he asked, that a group of ten terrorists were threatening to explode a nuclear device in St Peter's unless the pope gave them the Pieta?'"

"Paolo, rumors become more fanciful with every telling. Five terrorists become ten and eight million euros become the Pieta."

"You are right, Holy Father. Just after I had convinced my second friend there was no nuclear weapon in the church, he calls me back and asks me if the threat was not from a bomb but from anthrax. Then he asks me whether a group of radical feminists dressed as nuns had infiltrated the basilica and were distributing flyers and pamphlets supporting abortions and women priests."

"Paolo, throw these musicians out of the basilica. They have caused enough aggravation for one day."

"Holy Father, I would think twice before throwing them out."

"Why, Paolo?"

"The press will pillory you. The morning headlines will say that Pope Linus throws saints out of St. Peter's."

"You are right, Paolo. What should we do with them? The Swiss Guards have locked them in the sacristy."

"Have the guards release the musicians and escort them to the high altar. Give them your papal blessing, and promise to arrange a concert in the Vatican at some mutually convenient time next year. That should soothe any bruised feelings."

"Do as you wish, Remigi, but my miter is missing. Who has it? I will not walk down the aisle without it."

Remigi tried to calm the pope. Just then, a Swiss Guard whispered in Remigi's ear.

"Crisis averted, Holy Father. We've found your miter. A new bishop from Austria was trying it on for size."

After Pope Linus had imparted his blessing to everyone in the basilica, Bishop Patti escorted the Gospel singers down the center aisle to a virtuoso performance by the Vatican organist. Behind them walked the newly ordained bishops. As Patti reached the entrance to the basilica, he signaled the Swiss Guards to push open the bronze doors of the basilica. The morning rain had gone, and St. Peter's Square was bathed in brilliant sunshine.

Bishop Harbinger walked to where Pope Linus was standing, waiting to recess out of the basilica.

"Holy Father, I hope you liked the musicians and the singers. I don't know how Vincent found them."

The pope controlled his anger. "Thank your brother for his thoughtfulness."

"You might like to meet Vincent. He owns a nightclub in Harlem. If you ever visit New York City, I can take you there. It's called The Conclave."

"I have no plans to travel to New York in the foreseeable future, Bishop Harbinger."

"Well then, can I talk to you for a moment about a separate matter, Holy Father? Given all you must do, your mind must be pulled in all directions. Do you have enough time to pray and meditate? Do you ever have time just to sit quietly in an empty room?"

Pope Linus was incredulous. "Let me be clear about this. You are barely a bishop fifteen minutes and you want to talk to me about *my* spiritual life?"

"Yes, Holiness. Just for a few minutes. From my experience, once the day gets started, it becomes impossible to find time to relax, let alone meditate. The trick is to meditate before the day begins. Take a walk in the Vatican Gardens before you say Mass or have your first appointment. That's where a dog comes in."

"A dog!"

"Yes, a dog makes a wonderful companion. They say you have high blood pressure, Holy Father. Taking a dog for morning and evening walks will be good for your health."

"Thank you for your concern, Bishop Harbinger. But right now, no animals, including dogs, are permitted in the Vatican. Now if you'll excuse me."

"Holiness, change that rule. People will understand. You are under terrible stress. Having a dog is cheaper than paying for a new conclave to elect your successor."

The pope glowered at Harbinger.

"Excuse me, Your Excellency. If you wish to discuss the matter, see Monsignor Remigi to schedule an appointment—say in a month or two."

"But I'll be back in Lipoppo by then."

The pope began to walk down the aisle.

"Well then, perhaps you can make an appointment for the next time you're in Rome. Remigi will book far ahead."

It had been an eventful day in St. Peter's, but one thing had not changed. The number of reported pickpockets in the basilica remained virtually the same as the day before.

Chapter Three
Gabriel and His Elephants

After changing into one of the brightly colored dashikis that he had brought from Lipoppo, Samuel Harbinger threw his bishop's cassock over his arm and hurried out into St. Peter's Square in search of his luncheon companion, Ignatius Cropsy. Harbinger stood in the shade of the dome to keep from squinting from the bright sunlight. He could not see Father Cropsy's mane of red hair anywhere among the crowd. As Harbinger stood wondering how long to wait, he saw an elegantly dressed woman storm out of the basilica entrance.

He walked over to her as she angrily lit a cigarette. "What's wrong, ma'am? Can I help?"

"These Nazis at the door won't let me in the cathedral. First, they said my skirt was too short. When I tied my jacket around my waist to cover my legs, they said my arms were too bare. I let fly a few well-chosen words and left."

"What did you say to them?"

"Words a priest shouldn't hear."

Harbinger smiled.

"Can you get different clothes and come back tomorrow?"

"No. I'm here from Norway on business. My plane leaves for Oslo at eight o'clock tonight. I took some time off to run over here and see the Pieta."

"What's your name?"

"Hagerbloom. Christina Hagerbloom."

"Put this on, Christina." Harbinger handed the woman his bishop's cassock. "I am pretty short, but it should be long enough to cover you."

"Thank you, Father." Christina Hagerbloom's face beamed. "You're a godsend. I still may get to see the Pieta."

Harbinger watched as Christina Hagerbloom buttoned up the cassock. Throwing a military salute to her benefactor, she marched boldly up to the front door of the basilica. An usher went to stop her but then seemed to have second thoughts and waved her inside.

As Harbinger stood waiting for Christina to return the cassock, he saw Ignatius Cropsy running across St. Peter's Square.

"Sorry I'm late, Samuel, or must I now call you Bishop Harbinger."

"Samuel's still okay, Ignatius. By the way, thanks for getting me a slot to say Mass at the Clementine."

Cropsy laughed. "It must have been divine intervention. I walked into the scheduling office as the phone was ringing with a cancellation at the Clementine. And now, let me thank you for something."

"For what?"

"For giving me the opportunity to ride your bicycle in from the airport. It was great fun. To be honest, I haven't had as good a time in a long while. I'm going to buy a bike and ride it to work." Cropsy grinned. "Pedestrians of Rome beware. But in the meantime, let's have lunch."

"Give me a minute, Ignatius. I have to wait until Christina returns my cassock."

"What do you mean 'until Christina returns your cassock'?"

"The woman's skirt was above the knee. The ushers wouldn't let her into the church."

"So?"

"So I loaned her my cassock. All she wanted was to see the Pieta."

Cropsy gulped. "You lent this Christina woman your bishop's cassock—the one with the purple trim on it?"

"Yes. She was in Rome on business and could only take an hour off. She would never have gotten in to see the Pieta unless I loaned her my cassock."

"The powers-that-be around here frown on letting cross-dressers into the cathedral. They think it's disrespectful. Can you imagine how they'll react to a woman wearing a bishop's cassock? Good intentions are no defense."

Just then, Christina Hagerbloom, wearing the borrowed cassock, was marched out of the basilica by two grim-faced ushers dressed in dark suits and dark sunglasses. As they walked into the sunlight, the woman pointed sheepishly at Bishop Harbinger.

The ushers walked to where Samuel Harbinger was standing. "You are new here at the Vatican." The older of the two men spoke in a clipped, business-like tone.

"Yes. The pope ordained me a bishop earlier today."

"Giving a bishop's cassock to a woman so she can get into St. Peter's is a bit unorthodox, don't you think? I'm sorry, Your Excellency, I do not know your name."

"Samuel Harbinger, bishop of Lipoppo in Kenya. The cassock satisfies the dress code, doesn't it?"

"Yes, but you let a woman wear your bishop's cassock into the church."

"Sometimes if Bagua, my housekeeper, forgets to launder my vestments, I have to borrow a clean shirt from a neighbor so I can go into church and say Mass. Can't someone borrow my cassock to go into St. Peter's to see the Pieta?"

"But the someone is a woman! I can't comment on what

you do in Africa, Bishop Harbinger, but here in Rome, letting a woman borrow a bishop's cassock so she can enter the basilica is against the rules. We'll have to confiscate your cassock."

Bishop Harbinger walked over to Christina Hagerbloom.

"Give me the cassock, Christina. Pope Linus made me a bishop, and I will return it only to him." Harbinger stared defiantly at the two ushers. "If you want this cassock, you'll have to fight me for it."

The two ushers hesitated. Provoking a fight in the middle of St. Peter's Square would not be well received by the ushers' superiors.

"Keep your cassock," said one of the men. "But we will have to report your conduct to the appropriate authorities."

"Do what you must!"

The ushers walked away with self-righteous looks on their faces.

Cropsy howled in delight. "Bravo. You were great, Samuel. You stood up to those clothes police. If they had their way, they'd require women to wear full-length burkas to get into the basilica."

"And probably carry lit candles as well." Harbinger's eyes twinkled.

Cropsy roared with laughter.

"C'mon, Samuel. You are a breath of fresh air around here. I'll treat you to the best lunch in Rome."

Christina quickly refreshed her lipstick. "I guess I don't have much standing in this group, but could I please join you? I'm embarrassed at what happened. They threatened to take me to the Vatican police if I didn't cooperate. I just couldn't miss my eight o'clock flight to Oslo."

Harbinger smiled and patted her on the shoulder. "Don't worry about it, Christina. The important thing in all this is that you were able to see the Pieta. Sure, you can join us for lunch."

Cropsy listened in mock horror. "Before saying 'yes' to Christina, Samuel, don't you think you should find out whether a bishop can have lunch with a woman, and if he can, whether he can drink wine with her?"

"Ignatius, what possible objection can there be to having lunch with a woman?"

"Theologians can be inventive. The lunch might be viewed as a near occasion of sin."

Harbinger roared with laughter. "Christina, are you a near occasion of sin?"

"I don't think so, but I guess I should know what it is before I answer 'no.'"

"It's something that a Catholic must avoid because it most certainly will lead to sin. Cropsy, do you think Christina is a near occasion of sin?"

"No, but I guess she could be a remote occasion of sin."

"But I learned in the seminary that you don't have to avoid a remote occasion of sin."

"That's right. So let's go have lunch."

"I have a credit card." Christina took her wallet out of her purse.

"And I know the place." Cropsy pointed toward the Borgo Santo Spiritu.

"I hope the trattoria is full of Vatican dignitaries." Harbinger chuckled.

"I'll guarantee it'll be jam packed with them."

"Let's go then." Christina waved her credit card like a flag.

"And after lunch, Samuel, are we still on for my church-by-church tour of Rome?"

"Yes, as long as it includes the Biopark. Don't forget I want to see a tiger."

"I haven't forgotten, Samuel."

And so the three went off to have some fettuccine and wine and to be the subject of delicious gossip.

* * * * *

After an afternoon of visits to churches and several famous fountains in Rome, Cropsy and Harbinger finally reached the Biopark. Unfortunately, the tiger exhibit was closed for restoration. A disappointed Harbinger had hardly returned to the Domus when his phone rang.

"Did the pope like the gift?"

Samuel recognized his brother's voice.

"Yes, he said I should thank you for your thoughtfulness. How did you get the musicians and singers to Rome so fast?"

"A regular customer in the club loaned me his corporate jet. I rounded up a few out-of-work musicians—someone on banjo, trombone, drum, and two on trumpets. I added in a few singers. Then I flew them all to Rome. They practiced on the plane."

"Thanks, Vincent. You were a godsend."

"I hope you're still not having misgivings about becoming a bishop?"

"I guess every once in awhile I still have bouts of anxiety. Yesterday, a cardinal scolded me publicly for allowing children to bring their animals to Mass. I did not like being a bishop then."

"Who is this guy? I could have him roughed up a bit in some dark alley in Rome."

"Things are not done this way in the Vatican, big brother."

"Well, if you should ever change your mind, just give me a call."

* * * * * *

With his two hands clasped behind his back, an angry Pope Linus paced up and down his study. Cardinal Jensen and Monsignor Remigi stood quietly near trhe door.

"Can you believe this Bishop Harbinger pulling me off the papal throne and forcing me to dance with him? Jensen, you are the prefect of the Congregation for Bishops. You have jurisdiction over the appointment process. How did this Harbinger get chosen a bishop?"

"I don't have an answer, Your Holiness. It's being investigated."

Sister Consuela, the pope's housekeeper, slipped quietly into the room carrying a tray.

"Ah, my medicine has arrived. I seem to have prescriptions for everything, don't I, Sister Consuela?"

"Not for everything, Holiness. You only take five pills."

"Let me see if I can remember what they're for. The white pill is for high blood pressure. The dark blue pill is for high cholesterol. The purple pill is for acid reflux. The light blue pill is for arthritis. The red pill is for something, but I'm not exactly sure what."

"Holiness, it's a special multivitamin."

"Thank you, Sister."

Taking a mouthful of water, Pope Linus swallowed the five tablets.

"Consuela won't leave the room until I've finished taking all five pills. She's stubborn. Once she sat through a private conversation with the Spanish prime minister because I balked at taking one of my pills. I forgot which one it was."

Sister Consuela blushed. "Holiness, it was your blood pressure pill."

"Okay, Sister, I'm done and I didn't hide any pills in my desk drawer."

The housekeeper picked up the tray and started to leave the room. "The blood pressure pill must be taken twice a day, Holy Father. I'll bring you the second tablet after dinner."

When the nun left the room, Remigi resumed the conversation. "Holy Father, this Harbinger fellow meant no harm. He just got carried away. For a bishop from Africa, walking into St. Peter's for the first time must be a bit overwhelming."

"But the insolence of the man! A bishop fifteen minutes and he wants to know about my spiritual life—whether I spend enough time in prayer and meditation."

"Holy Father, the man has a point. You barely have time to say

Mass let alone read a book. As for meditation, when was the last time you spent quiet time in your chapel?"

"Okay, Harbinger may be right on that, Remigi. But then he started talking about getting a dog. He thinks a dog would be good for my mental and physical health. Since when is he my doctor?"

"Holy Father, this Harbinger is right. You do not get any exercise. Walking a dog every morning and evening would make sure you got at least some exercise. You do have high blood pressure. I think you take the round white pill for it."

"Paolo, how can you defend this Harbinger? He's arrogant."

"Holiness, you've met this man. How can you call him arrogant? He is simple and God-fearing."

Pope Linus scowled. "What do you mean 'simple and God-fearing'?"

"He brings a gift to thank you for making him a bishop. Why? I'm sure it was something his parents taught him to do. He speaks what's in his heart because he knows no other way to speak. And he tries to help people. See how he helped that Dutch bishop prostrate himself. There's something about the man that's appealing—it's almost a feeling of saintliness."

"Saintliness?"

"Yes, you feel happy when you are with him."

Cardinal Jensen shook his head in disbelief. "Don't tell me that Monsignor Remigi is trying to convince us that this Harbinger is a modern day Saint Francis of Assisi? He did tame a lion, at least so he says, and Francis, the infamous wolf of Gubbio. But there the resemblance stops."

Pope Linus sat down behind his desk.

"Tell me how you see him, Jensen."

"Harbinger's wily and manipulative. He apes loyalty to the teaching authority of the church while championing his own views of how the church should function."

"How can you say that, Your Eminence?" Remigi glared at Jensen.

"Take off your rose-tinted glasses, Remigi, and look at three issues. First, Harbinger lends his bishop's cassock to a woman so she can get into St. Peter's."

"The woman wanted to see the Pieta—it was nothing more sinister than that."

"I disagree. By helping this woman, he was sending a message of support to women's rights' groups in the church. Second, he lets children bring their animals to Mass."

"Your Eminence, this policy that you criticize seems to have doubled the number of children attending Sunday Mass in his village of Lipoppo. Count the number of children at Sunday Mass in a typical church here in Rome. You'll be lucky if you find anyone under sixty."

"No matter how many more children come to Mass, Remigi, animals should not be allowed in church. They distract from the liturgy. Imagine praying standing next to a horse. The thought is ludicrous."

Remigi picked up the cudgels. "But as a church, Jensen, shouldn't we be taking steps to encourage the next generation of Catholics to attend Mass and take the Eucharist?"

Pope Linus interrupted. "Remigi, I think Jensen is right on this. People come to church for quiet and a place to talk with God. They should not have to compete with noisy animals. For the future, however, the church should explore ways to allow animals to participate in church services without creating a disturbance. In this context, we must always remember that animals do have souls. They are a part of God's creation."

"Holiness, I think it's better to have an absolute ban on animals in church."

"No, Jensen, let's leave some room to experiment on these issues. I have worked hard to create a cadre of well-trained bishops. They should begin to develop balanced solutions on these matters. Now what is your third issue, Eminence?"

"Harbinger has been invited to speak at the Gregorian

University tomorrow at noon. And we all know who runs the Gregorian. The Jesuits!"

Pope Linus looked startled. "Is this true, Remigi? Have the Jesuits invited him to speak at the Gregorian tomorrow?"

"Yes, Holiness. They have."

The pope slammed his fist on the desk sending a pencil flying halfway across the room.

"Leave it to the Jesuits to cozy up to this Harbinger. If the Jesuits have invited him, they must know that he'll say something controversial. Send Mabibin to the speech, Jensen, and make sure he takes his pad and pencil. I want him to take detailed notes. With the Jesuits involved, I may have to add another pill to my collection of medicines."

"I will send Mabibin, Holy Father. He is also checking how Harbinger ever became a bishop." Cardinal Jensen bowed and started to leave the pope's study. "Oh. I forgot one thing more. Do you know what Harbinger asked me?"

"What?"

"He asked why Michelangelo had not painted black men or women in his frescoes. What a silly remark."

Jensen left the room. Pope Linus slumped back into his chair.

"Paolo, what should we do with this Harbinger? He shows no respect for the institutions of the church. If anything, his attitude is a threat."

"Change usually starts as a threat, Holy Father."

"I know that, Paolo."

"Holiness, you are a Basque and this Harbinger is a Kenyan. You should be friends—you are both outsiders in the church."

"Let's wait and see what Harbinger says at the Gregorian."

* * * * * *

Two near accidents and one flat tire later, Harbinger and Cropsy pedaled their way through the gates of Gregorian

University. Parked in the courtyard was a Mercedes Benz sedan with red and white license plates marked SCV 4.

"That's Jensen's car." Cropsy looked at his watch. "It's only eleven AM. He's here early."

As one might have predicted, there was standing room only in the main auditorium of the Gregorian. Rank normally has its privileges but not today. Bishops who came late had to stand in the back with students and members of the press. While Harbinger waited for the rector of the university to introduce him, he leaned over and whispered in Father Cropsy's ear.

"Where's Cardinal Jensen sitting, Ignatius? I don't see him."

Cropsy looked out across the crowd. Suddenly he blanched.

"Jensen didn't come. He sent Mabibin instead and in the cardinal's car no less."

"Who's Mabibin?"

"Jensen's assistant. If there were anybody at the Vatican who could be called 'shadowy,' it would be Mabibin. He could find heresy in the words of the *Pater Noster*."

"Where is he sitting?"

"He's that tall, somber-looking priest near the back door. Be careful what you say. I'm sure Jensen has sent him here to cause trouble. Mabibin'll carefully scrutinize every word you say and every assertion you make."

Minutes later, the door to the lecture hall flew open. An apologetic and out-of-breath rector hurried up to the podium.

"*Mea culpa*. Even by Rome's normal standards, today is a busy day on the streets. I finally parked my car and walked."

The rector took out a piece of paper from his vest pocket. "I am happy to be here today to welcome Bishop Harbinger to the 'Greg.' Few people have captured the imagination of the Vatican as quickly as this man has. The picture in the newspaper of his dancing with Pope Linus will be long remembered. Someone said that joy and happiness are forms of self-healing. Self-healing is what is needed in our church today. Perhaps this bishop from the village of Lipoppo in Kenya can teach us how to go about that process. Without further delay, let me introduce to you Bishop Samuel Harbinger. His remarks are entitled, Jesus' Message in Today's World."

"Thank you, Father Rector. Even in my village of Lipoppo, we have heard of the Jesuit Order and its many accomplishments."

Harbinger stopped for a minute while a technician turned up the volume of the sound system. When the technician had finished, Harbinger continued.

"I come here from Africa. As Father Rector has told you, from the village of Lipoppo in Kenya." Bishop Harbinger nervously held the microphone in his right hand. "Jesus' message to the human race is direct and simple—love God and love your neighbor. In Lipoppo, it is easy to live out Jesus' message. Obani, the village postman, comes every day and knocks on your door whether you have mail or not. Why? Because he cares for everyone in the village and wants to make sure everybody is well. Obani is God's messenger. Then there is Miriam. She is an elderly woman. No one knows how old she is. She goes every day to the AIDS clinic to help the dying. Like Obani, Miriam is God's messenger. We have many Obani's and Miriam's in Lipoppo.

"In a busy city like Rome; however, it is more difficult to live out Jesus' message. Before he came to Lipoppo, the postman Obani had worked in Kinshasa. There were so many people on his mail route that he could only stop at houses when there was mail to be delivered. Obani did not have time to stop at the others.

"In Lipoppo, we say that when life is simple, we kneel on the ground and speak openly to God, but when life becomes crowded, we must learn to kneel upright and speak to God silently.

"Pope Linus is a holy and virtuous man. As Supreme Pontiff of the Catholic Church, he has the responsibility to bring God's message to Catholics throughout the world—whether they live in my village of Lipoppo or in Rome, Nairobi, or New York. But he needs all of us in this room to assist him in governing the church. We must become Obanis and Miriam's. God calls each and every one of us to share the pope's responsibilities—in essence, to become co-popes."

The Bishop of Lipoppo walked off the platform to thunderous applause. "How did I do, Ignatius?"

"The stories about Obani and Miriam were great, but I don't know about the co-pope stuff. I saw Mabibin furiously scribbling notes. He filled up several pages of his notepad."

* * * * * *

A waiter walked to a private room where a group of prelates and Vatican officials were dining.

"Cardinal Jensen, there's a phone call for you from Father Mabibin."

"Tell him I'll speak to him tomorrow."

"He says it's urgent."

Annoyed, Jensen got up from the table and excused himself. The waiter escorted the cardinal to a private phone.

"Mabibin, was it necessary to call me here at this time of night?"

"Yes, Your Eminence, it was."

"Well then, get on with it. I assume you're calling me about this Samuel Harbinger?"

"Yes. There are actually two Samuel Harbingers and the wrong one was made a bishop."

"So he was a mistake!"

"Yes."

"How did this happen?"

"I'm not sure. As best as I can tell, a letter was supposed to be sent to Father Samuel Harbinger inviting him to come to Rome to be ordained bishop of the French town of Lepeaupeaux. Don't ask me how, but the letter was addressed by accident to a different Father Samuel Harbinger inviting him to come to Rome to be ordained bishop of the Kenyan village of Lipoppo."

"If this French Father Harbinger knew he had been named a

bishop, wouldn't he have checked on the status of his episcopal appointment? He should have discovered the mistake."

"Normally this would have happened."

"What do you mean 'normally'?"

"Just around this time, the French Harbinger was killed in a car accident. For a period of months, our office was not informed of the accident. When we did learn of it, we said nothing."

"Why the secrecy?"

"It seems there was a passenger in the car with the French Father Harbinger—a local prostitute. I should amend what I just said—a local prostitute carrying Harbinger's baby. To avoid scandal, our nuncio in France said nothing. The French Harbinger's episcopal appointment died. The Kenyan Harbinger's episcopal appointment, on the other hand, went through without objection."

"But didn't this Harbinger have to be vetted through our apostolic nuncio in Kenya? He would have discovered the problem."

"Because the Kenyan Harbinger was never an official candidate for the episcopacy, the nuncio never got involved in the selection process."

"So what you're telling me, Mabibin, is that this Kenyan Samuel Harbinger somehow fell through the cracks and was ordained a bishop yesterday."

"Yes, I think so, Your Eminence. In all my years working here at the congregation, I have never seen a situation like this before."

"The pope will be furious. You know that one of his top priorities is choosing the best-qualified priests as bishops. Can we relieve this Harbinger of his episcopal powers?"

"No, Your Eminence, unless he preaches heresy, we can't undo our mistake. He is a canonically consecrated bishop in the line of apostolic succession."

"What about his talk today at the Gregorian?"

"He spoke about the concept of a 'co-pope.'"

"Sounds heretical to me, Mabibin."

"Perhaps. But there's at least one piece of good news, Eminence."

"What's that?"

"I don't think the church would be liable for the woman's shawl. There's a doctrine called the assumption of the risk. The woman came to Mass knowing the monkey would be there. She assumed the risk of normal animal behavior."

"Small consolation, Mabibin."

* * * * * *

"Holy Father." Jensen stood in front of the pope's desk like a penitent boy about to be chastised. "Harbinger was mistakenly selected to become a bishop, but he was validly ordained."

"How did this happen?"

"A French priest named Samuel Harbinger was supposed to be ordained, but a Kenyan priest with the same name was ordained in his place. I'll take responsibility for the mistake my office made. It was slipshod practice. There's no way to sugarcoat it."

Pope Linus angrily threw down his pencil on his desk. "So Harbinger somehow did fall through the cracks, is that what you're telling me, Jensen?"

"Yes, Your Holiness. He should not have been made a bishop. He was a mistake."

"There must be a way to relieve this Harbinger of his episcopal powers."

"Unfortunately, there isn't, Holiness. We made the mistake in ordaining him. He did not seek the job—he did not deceive or defraud us. He's a priest and old enough to be ordained a bishop. Nothing can change the facts."

"Is this true, Mabibin?"

"Yes, Holy Father."

"So I am infallible and an absolute monarch to boot, but

I'm powerless to strip this Bishop Harbinger of his episcopal powers?"

"That's right. He was validly ordained. The only thing we can do is accuse him of heresy, convict him, and then excommunicate him. It would be a long, drawn-out procedure. He would have the right to refute the charges lodged against him. It would get messy."

"What did he say at the Gregorian, Mabibin?"

"He spoke of co-popes."

"I have heard of anti-popes but never co-popes. Are you sure he used the word 'co-pope,' Mabibin?"

"Yes, Holiness." Mabibin flipped open his notepad. "His exact words were, and I quote, 'God calls each and every one of us to share the pope's responsibilities—in essence to become 'co-popes.'"

Pope Linus grew angry. "This is outrageous. I don't remember Jesus saying 'You are Peter and upon you and everyone else, I will build my church.' Any third grade catechism teacher would say this co-pope idea is bad theology."

Paolo Remigi opened his attaché case. "Before you label Bishop Harbinger a heretic, Holiness, you should be aware of how he is being received in the press."

"What do you mean, Paolo?"

"The good bishop has become a celebrity overnight. The press loves him—pictures of the two of you dancing in St. Peter's have made the front page of virtually every newspaper in the world. The Italian papers are outdoing themselves. *La Stampa* in Turin has a headline that reads, 'Miracle in St. Peter's.' *Il Messaggero* says simply 'WOW.'"

"What do the British papers say?"

"The headline in *The Times of London* reads, 'Rollicking Good Time in St. Peter's.' *The Guardian* was a little more titillating. 'All Hell Breaks Loose in St. Peter's.' I even saw a paper from your native city of Bilbao."

"What did it say?"

"Pope Basques in New Light."

Pope Linus poured himself a glass of water.

"So what you're saying Paolo, is that far from humiliating me, this Lipoppo is enhancing my image?"

"Yes, Holy Father, dancing on the altar has 'humanized' you. It's made you a more sympathetic figure. You're not the 'Somber Pontiff' anymore."

"But what about the word, 'co-pope'?"

"I received an e-mail from Richard Plimpton, the archbishop of New York, with regard to the use of this term."

"What did Cardinal Plimpton have to say?" The pope opened a pad to jot down notes.

"He says he has called several bishops in the United States to ask what they think about Harbinger's 'co-pope' remark. In his words, the reaction has been overwhelmingly positive. His advice would be to endorse the concept in the most general terms and say nothing more."

"Does Plimpton suggest any language?"

"Yes. I'll quote it exactly—the laity and the papacy are two sides of a coin—you can't have the one without the other. In this sense, the pope and the laity are already co-popes sharing in the governance of the church. The idea of a 'co-pope' is merely a restatement, not a reevaluation of existing church teaching."

Pope Linus smiled broadly.

"No matter what the problem, Richard Plimpton always points out that the solution has been staring us in the face for a long time. We just haven't recognized it as a solution until now."

Jensen growled scornfully. "Plimpton may be clever with words, but he is not much of a theologian. What does he mean by saying Harbinger's use of the term 'co-pope' is merely a restatement, not a reevaluation of church teaching? We should come down hard against this notion."

The pope poured himself another glass of water.

"Jensen, Plimpton's a shrewd politician and a master of the nuance. You should always listen to his input. Let's do what he proposes and release a statement along the lines he suggests. If Plimpton says bishops in the United States are positive toward this 'co-pope' idea, then the statement will please the American hierarchy. We are always saying 'no' to them. Here's the chance to say 'yes.'"

"As you wish, Holy Father." Jensen left the room, his anger walking beside him.

* * * * * *

The next day a telephone call came from Lipoppo.

"This is Obani, the postman, calling for Bishop Harbinger."

"Obani, this is Samuel. Is there a problem in the village?"

"Yes. Someone threw a dead carcass into the well on the outskirts of Woomba. It will take three days for the water to become safe to drink. In the meantime, Father Albert asks if Woomba's shepherds can water their flocks at our well. Should we allow them to do it?"

"Obani, what would Jesus have done?" Harbinger knew that the whole village of Lipoppo was most likely crowded around the phone in the post office, trying to hear the conversation.

"He would let them water their sheep."

"Then we should do so as well."

There was a pause on the line.

"Obani, do you have something else to ask me?"

"We saw the story in the newspaper about you becoming a bishop."

"Yes, I know. Did the newspaper send the village many copies?"

"Yes. Everyone who could read was given one."

"Good! Obani, take one to Father Albert in Woomba."

"I will, Bishop Samuel. The picture in the newspaper showed you dancing with the pope. Do you go dancing often in Rome?"

Now Harbinger knew the reason for the phone call. The

question about the well was only a pretext. The call was about when he was coming home.

"Tell the village I'll be home in two weeks, Obani. Sooner if possible."

"Bishop Harbinger, before you hang up, there is someone else who wishes to say hello to you."

"Who is it?"

"Give us a moment to bring him to the phone."

Bishop Samuel heard some scuffling at the end of the phone line.

"Okay, Bishop, your friend is on the line. Say something to him."

"This is Samuel Harbinger. To whom am I speaking?"

When Banda heard Samuel's voice, he looked quizzically at the phone and began to purr loudly.

"Is that you, Banda?"

The lion growled and tried to bite the phone.

Obani took the receiver away from Banda's ear.

"We had better not let this go on too long, Bishop Harbinger. Banda seems to be getting confused. He doesn't understand a telephone. He hears you, but he cannot see you."

"How did you get him to come to the telephone?"

"Bagua fed him a mixture of herbs that made him groggy. Mobeki and Hestern loaded him onto the Jeep and drove him here to the post office."

Samuel Harbinger choked with emotion when he put down the phone.

* * * * * *

That night Bishop Harbinger rode his bicycle out into the vastness of St. Peter's Square. The phone call from Lipoppo had made him homesick. He wanted a quiet place to say the rosary before he went to sleep. A woman who owned one of the tourist shops near the square recognized him. She pulled out a set of beads from her purse and joined him in praying the rosary. Soon the number of those saying the rosary grew to five, then to ten, then to a hundred. Gusts of wind carried the prayers of the faithful out across the city.

The next night, Father Cropsy decided to accompany his friend. It was a good thing he did. Thanks to a story in *Il Messaggero* about the bishop's midnight rosary, more than a thousand people turned up in front of the basilica—some out of curiosity, some out of devotion. After saying the rosary, the crowd milled about in a festive mood.

A young student held up a makeshift placard. "Tell us a story about Lipoppo," it read.

Bishop Harbinger smiled when he saw the sign.

"What is your name, my son, and where are you from?"

"My name is Tomas Brandzek, and I'm from Schenectady."

"Schenectady? Where's that?"

"It's a city in New York."

"I would like to visit Schenectady some day. It may be like Lipoppo."

"But we have no lions or elephants in Schenectady, Bishop Harbinger. Tell us about them. You must have many stories."

"Yes. I will tell you a story about Gabriel and his elephants, but then I must go to sleep."

Many in the crowd sat on the ground. Father Cropsy found a wooden box for his diminutive friend to stand on so everyone could see him.

"When he was eight years old, Gabriel was crippled by polio," the bishop began. "The boy had no friends except his elephants. Every morning just after dawn, Gabriel would take his cane and hobble to the water hole. There he would sit talking to his friends. Every now and then, one of the elephants would kneel in front of Gabriel so the boy could pull out nettles that had stuck in the elephant's hide. If he found a place where a nettle had caused infection, Gabriel would apply a poultice made from a plant that grows along the water's edge. Gabriel even learned how to treat parasites that bore into the elephants' iron-hard feet. The townspeople shook their heads. 'Poor Gabriel,' they would say. 'He has nobody but the elephants.'

"Then last year the fire came. The wind blew the flames toward Lipoppo. The water trucks would not arrive for at least three hours. The townspeople gathered their possessions and prepared to flee. Gabriel came to me. 'Father Harbinger, the elephants can use their trunks to spray water on the fire. They can hold back the flames until the trucks arrive, but the villagers must help. An elephant's eyes are weak. They need to be shown where the fire is burning.'

"I gathered a group of villagers and ran to the water hole. Gabriel gently put a rope around the neck of each animal. 'Hold one of these ropes, each one of you. Use it to guide the elephant from the water hole to the flames. He will not hurt you. I have told them what we must do.'"

The bishop's eyes filled with tears as he remembered that night.

"Gabriel, the crippled boy whom the villagers said would never amount to anything, saved Lipoppo from destruction. God has a plan for all of us. Now I must go. It is late."

"No. No. Tell us another story about Gabriel and his animals." Tomas Brandzek, the student from Schenectady, was persistent.

"Tomas, I promise to tell you another story, but not tonight. I am tired."

As Harbinger got on his bicycle to leave, Brandzek pointed to the fourth floor windows of the Apostolic Palace. There was a light on in the pope's study.

"Look, the Holy Father is still up. Let's invite him down to the square to hear the story of Gabriel and the elephants."

Brandzek ran under the windows and started to call out the pope's name. Soon more and more people joined in the clamor. Suddenly, the shutters opened and a smiling Pope Linus appeared at the window The Holy Father held up his hands to quiet the crowd in the square.

"The police have told me you are too loud. It is late. Go home to your families."

"Holy Father, Bishop Harbinger has just told us a story about a young boy named Gabriel and his elephants. Together they saved the village of Lipoppo from burning to the ground. Come down and hear the story." Brandzek was insistent.

"No. I must go back to work. Perhaps tomorrow I can hear it." The pope blessed the crowd, pulled the shutters tight, and walked back into his study.

The pope's appearance had emboldened the crowd. Several women found whistles in their purses and started blowing them. Then a nearby taxi began to sound its horn. After five minutes, the shutters opened again and the pope came back to the window. This time Cardinal Jensen was at his side.

"You are stubborn," cried Pope Linus. "I have asked Cardinal Jensen to come down and meet with you."

A woman dressed smartly in a dark blue coat shook her head. "No, we want you, Holy Father. The Bishop of Lipoppo is here and will tell you the story."

Cardinal Jensen looked at the pope and shook his head vehemently.

"You cannot go out into the square at night, Holy Father. The Swiss Guards will not allow it. It's a question of security."

"Jensen, let me speak to the officer in charge."

Minutes later, Jensen returned with a rather nervous Swiss Guard.

"Holy Father, is there a problem?"

"I don't think so, Officer. Could you open St. Peter's for me without compromising security? I wish to speak with a group of pilgrims."

"Holy Father, there would be no problem as long as you stayed inside the basilica."

"Then, Officer, open St. Peter's for me."

Cardinal Jensen looked horrified. "Your Holiness, I advise you against ..."

"I'm going, Jensen, and that's that. Whether I like it or not, this Lipoppo is a bishop of the church. Your office saw to that. I should not hide from him."

* * * * * *

As several members of the Swiss Guard pushed open the bronze doors to St. Peter's, an excited Father Cropsy whispered in his friend's ear. "I can't believe this is really happening."

"Ignatius, maybe this is the signal from Pope Linus that you've been waiting for."

The officer in charge motioned the crowd to come into the basilica.

"Remember, photos are permitted, but please, no audio recordings."

A physically challenged woman in an electric cart raised her hand.

"Officer, will you let this contraption into the church?"

"Of course, but no using the horn."

The woman smiled. "You have my promise. And I hope my blind friend over there can bring his guide dog in with him."

"Yes, as long as he is kept on a leash and doesn't start barking." The Swiss Guard wagged his finger playfully at the dog. "Now if there are no more questions, let's not keep the Holy Father waiting."

The crowd walked down the center aisle. The pope came out of the sanctuary, wearing a green stole draped over his shoulders.

"I bid you all welcome. I was told I should hear a story about a boy named Gabriel and his herd of elephants."

Tomas Brandzek nodded his head. "Bishop Harbinger told the story to us. We want him to repeat it to you."

Pope Linus smiled politely. "The Good Bishop and I share one thing in common. We have both danced on the altar of this basilica. But come, Bishop, tell me this story of the boy Gabriel and his elephants."

* * * * * *

When Bishop Harbinger had finished recounting the tale of Gabriel and his herd of elephants, the pope stood up from his throne.

"This boy Gabriel was clearly an instrument of God. Maybe Gabriel would like to come to Rome. I would enjoy meeting him."

"Holy Father … that would not be possible."

"If money is a concern, Bishop Harbinger, the church will pay for the boy's trip."

"It is not money, Holy Father."

"Then what is it?"

"Gabriel is dead."

"Dead?"

"Yes, Holiness. He died of AIDS two months ago."

The pontiff slumped back into his throne, color draining from his face.

"I will remember Gabriel in my Mass tomorrow."

Cropsy whispered in Harbinger's ear. "You would think a pope could do a little better than 'I'll remember him at Mass tomorrow.' It sounds a bit perfunctory."

"Ignatius, what else could he have said? Anything would have fallen short."

Suddenly, the guide dog broke loose from his blind master, and dodging a Swiss Guard, scampered up the steps of the altar. The pope smiled as the dog jumped up and sat in his lap. When the pontiff petted him, the dog started to bark and lick the pope's hand.

The dog's master said, "Giorgio, stop barking or you'll have to leave the church."

The pope smiled. "That will not be necessary, sir. We'll make a one-time exception for allowing Giorgio to stay in the basilica despite his barking."

"Thank you, Holy Father," said the blind man.

"Tell me, sir, what breed of dog is Giorgio?"

"A corgi. The English royal family has bred them for decades."

"Bishop Harbinger told me I should have a dog. What do you say to that?"

"I think Bishop Harbinger is right. Giorgio brings me so much joy and happiness that I could not imagine life without him. Every morning and evening, we walk together. I can't walk very fast, but Giorgio stays with me. Your Holiness, I know you are the head of the Catholic Church. Many people work for you; your picture hangs in churches the world over, but do you have someone who cares for you not as a pope but as a person?"

Pope Linus looked at the blind man.

"You are an eloquent advocate for having a Giorgio in one's life."

The pope stood up to leave. He bent down and petted Giorgio on his head. "Remember next time you come in here—no barking."

Pope Linus walked into the sacristy and disappeared from view.

* * * * * *

The next morning, Bishop Harbinger was up early. He was scheduled to say Mass at the Clementine Chapel at eleven o'clock and meet Sergio Bonti for a late lunch. He knew Bonti would scold him for not having ordered name cards. Harbinger decided to dedicate the morning to finding a print shop.

He went into the restaurant at the Domus for a quick breakfast. Someone had hung a "Welcome Branch Managers" banner just outside the entrance to the dining room. Several staff members were perched on chairs taking it down.

"Why are these men removing the banner?" Harbinger asked his waiter.

"Cardinal Jensen ordered it taken down. He found the humor

offensive. The rumor is he called the manager of the Domus early this morning and told him to have it down by noon. No one likes to run afoul of Jensen, so my guess is that the manager will have it taken down long before midday. When you work here, you get used to Jensen's fiats—you accept them as a part of life. But enough about Jensen. What would you like for breakfast, Your Excellency?"

"Toast and coffee. By the way, could you tell me who is in charge of the Vatican switchboard? I forgot his name."

"Cesare Duo. He's the director of telecommunications here at the Vatican. The switchboard comes under his authority."

"Could you ask Signor Duo to join me for a cup of coffee?"

"Yes, of course. I'm sure he'll be right in. He is very punctual."

Minutes later, a rather plump man with thinning gray hair and small eyes sat down next to Bishop Harbinger. "I believe you wished to see me, Your Excellency."

"You must be Cesare Duo?"

"Yes."

The two men shook hands.

"Signor Duo, I wish to speak to you about a young man named Giovanni. I understand he works in the Vatican switchboard."

"Yes, his sister has AIDS. I'm always making exceptions for him. He either has an excuse for being late or a request for leaving early."

"Well, I am saying Mass at the Clementine Chapel at eleven this morning. I would like Giovanni to be my altar server."

"I see Giovanni has hoodwinked you, too. If I give him the time off, rest assured, he won't show up at your Mass. He'll be off somewhere making money. That's the way he is."

"I don't think so."

"Well, let's see who is right. I'll give Giovanni time off between ten and noon. Let's see if he shows up at your Mass."

"Thank you, Signor Duo. I'm going to send you some hippo stew as a thank you present."

"I do not accept gifts, Father Harbinger. Hipppo meat is no exception."

* * * * * *

After finishing his coffee, Harbinger walked up to the seminarian on duty at the front desk. "Could you recommend a print shop in the neighborhood?"

"Of course, Your Excellency. There's one about a thirty-minute walk from here. It specializes in clerical materials. Shall I call for a taxi?"

"No, I'll take my bicycle. I must get used to riding on the wrong side of the street. What's the name and address of the store?"

"It's called Dignitas." The priest wrote the address on a piece of paper. "It's just off the Piazza Navona. You can't miss it."

* * * * * *

When Harbinger reached the Piazza Navona, he stopped for a minute to watch the workers dismantling the Christmas Market that had been set up there for the holiday season. He marveled at the life-sized nativity scene that stood in the middle of the piazza.

Harbinger had no difficulty in finding Dignitas. The sign over the doorway glistened in the bright morning sunshine. Harbinger stood his bicycle up against the wall and went into the shop. An elderly man with a round face and oval-shaped eyes sat behind the counter reading a newspaper. He fidgeted with a pen as he read.

The man looked up when he heard the door open.

"Good morning, Bishop Harbinger. My name is Giuseppe Chimati, the proprietor of the store. The Chimati family has owned this business for over ninety years. We have done work for eight popes and numerous cardinals and bishops, both here and abroad. What can I do for you?"

"How did you know my name and rank, Signor Chimati?"

"It is my business to know everyone who comes into the store. Yesterday fifty-two new bishops were ordained. In the next week, just about all of them will come to Dignitas looking for something. I have everyone's picture. It only takes me a moment to recognize who it is coming through the door. Now tell me why you have come, Bishop Harbinger?"

"I am interested in buying name cards."

"Of course. Let me show you the choices. There are simple name cards, what used to be referred to as calling cards and business cards that are more elaborate. I have a wide selection of options within each category."

Chimati took a book down from a shelf. "Here are examples of name or calling cards. They contain the basics—name, address, and telephone number. Some customers like to have a devotional picture on the card, like a picture of the Virgin Mary or the Holy Ghost. We recommend the picture, but there are those who think it a bit tacky."

"And the business card?"

"Business cards are more elaborate. They contain the basics of the name card plus additional information such as fax numbers, e-mail addresses, memberships in military orders, and perhaps a picture of the client standing next to Pope Linus. We strongly recommend that if you have access to the Holy Father, you should show it on the business card."

"What are these military orders you speak of? Does the Vatican have an army?"

Chimati laughed. "No, the pope has no legions. Although someone may be called a Knight of Malta or a Knight of the Holy Sepulcher of Jerusalem, he doesn't fight, at least not with weapons."

"Then with what?"

"With a checkbook. Knights support hospitals and other charities throughout the world."

"Maybe a knight would bring his checkbook and come to live in Lipoppo?"

"I can't say. But getting back to name cards, can I make a suggestion about the type of card you should get?"

"Yes, of course."

"If you were a priest, I would recommend the calling card—keep it simple. But you are a bishop. I would recommend starting right off with the business card."

"Why?"

"Bishops are in the governance structure of the church. They are called into many more matters than priests are. Therefore, fax numbers and e-mail addresses become important."

"That makes sense, Signor Chimati."

"Good. Now let's design the card. First, we need your name and diocese in the center of the card."

Harbinger printed "Samuel Harbinger, Diocese of Lipoppo."

"Now I need you to print your home address, your telephone numbers—landline and cell—and e-mail address."

"What is a cell phone? Do you mean the phone that runs without electricity?"

"I guess you can call it that."

"I don't have one of these phones."

"Well, we can add a cell phone number later. Tell me, do you have an e-mail address?"

"I don't think so."

"Bishop Harbinger, it's time to get you into the twenty-first century."

Harbinger chuckled. "Must I? It's comfortable where I am now."

"Yes, you must. If you are going to advance up through the hierarchy, you must be computer literate to some degree."

"Oh, I forgot to include something, Mr. Chimati. I'd like to list one other phone number on my card."

"What number is that?"

"My brother Vincent's. He owns a nightclub in New York City called The Conclave. He's there all the time."

"It's a bit unusual to put the phone number of a nightclub in New York on a Kenyan bishop's business card, don't you think?"

"Not if it's my brother's number. He could track me down in an emergency."

"Okay. I assume you want your standard three and a half by two-inch white card with rank appropriate ink. As a bishop that would mean purple ink. We could use plain black ink, if you would prefer."

"No, purple is fine."

"We talked earlier about a devotional picture."

"A Virgin Mary with a dove sitting on her shoulder would be nice."

"Interesting touch—having the Holy Spirit sitting on Mary's shoulder."

"Thank you."

"Do you also want some printed announcements of your ordination as a bishop?"

"What would I do with them?"

"Take them back to Africa and send them out to family and friends. When you get a wedding announcement, what do you think of first?"

"That two of God's children have fallen in love and decided to have a family."

"Your Excellency, that's a bit old-fashioned. You must learn to think of a bishop's ordination as a wedding without a bride and groom. Looked at it in this way, the ordination announcement is a fancy type of gift solicitation, that's the long and short of it. You never know what you'll get. A wealthy friend might give you a chalice. Some bishops have told me they got lots of gift certificates from men's apparel stores. Bishops need clothes like everyone else. By the way, do you have a Starbucks in Lipoppo?"

"What's Starbucks?"

"Lipoppo must really be in the middle of nowhere if you don't have a Starbucks. It's an upscale coffee store. One bishop told me someone gave him a Starbucks' card with one hundred euros of credit. One thing is clear, unless you send out announcements, there won't be many gifts."

"The people of Lipoppo are poor. I will not send out these announcements asking for gifts."

"As you wish. By the way, you may not know it, but a bishop is entitled to have a coat of arms."

"No, thanks. Lipoppo is very warm. I never wear a coat, but thanks for asking."

"Just checking. We sell lots of coats of arms."

"Signor Chimati, when will the cards be ready?"

"In an hour. I should say there's another service the Chimati family provides for our clients, free of charge."

"What is it?"

"It's called career tracking. We'll keep you informed of job opportunities in the Vatican or other possibilities in Italy or abroad. We'll even call you if we think you should start spending more on clothes. We might recommend that you buy more tailored suits, for example. It's hard not having a wife."

* * * * * *

With his business cards in his pocket, Harbinger pedaled across St. Peter's Square. He hoped that Giovanni would come to the Clementine Chapel to be his altar server. When he reached the basilica, he hurried to the sacristy for robing. After putting his vestments on, Harbinger walked to the chapel. Several people had gathered near the door waiting for Mass to begin. When Giovanni saw Bishop Harbinger, he ran up to him.

"Signor Duo called and said I could have ten AM to noon off—something about new circuitry being installed. I called my brother and two sisters to come and meet me at your Mass. All three of them came."

Tears welled up in Giovanni's eyes. "Bishop Harbinger, could we serve the Mass together as a family?"

"I see no reason why not."

Bishop Harbinger made the sign of the cross and spoke the familiar Latin words that open the Mass. "*Introibo ad Altare Dei.* I will walk to the altar of God."

Giovanni responded.

"*Ad Deum Qui Laetificat Juventutem Meam.* To God who brings joy to my youth."

The bishop felt the presence of God close around him.

* * * * * *

Samuel Harbinger sat down in a chair across from Bonti. "I'm sorry I'm late for lunch, Sergio."

"Not to worry. I went ahead and ordered."

"Good."

"Samuel, you must be one happy man these last couple of days." Bonti laid a pile of newspapers on the table. "First, it was the dancing in St. Peter's, and last night the corgi sitting in the pope's lap. Keep this up and you'll need an agent to book your appearances."

"Talking to the pope in St. Peter's last night was an unforgettable experience, Sergio."

"I understand from your friend Father Cropsy ..."

"Sergio, I think his name is actually pronounced Cromsky."

"Whatever—Cromsky/Cropsy told me that you never got to see your tiger. The Biopark building that houses the tigers was closed for restoration. In Italy, you should not get your hopes up too high. Half of Italy is always being restored and is off limits to tourists."

"But the Biopark is planning to show a film about African water holes. You should make time to see it," the bishop encouraged.

"Why?"

"I know you are heavily involved in efforts to bring peace

to Jerusalem. If a zebra and a lion can work out rules to coexist peacefully at a water hole, an Arab and a Jew should be able to work out similar rules to coexist peacefully in Jerusalem."

Bonti laughed aloud. "An African water hole is not going to provide answers to the problems of a complex city like Jerusalem."

"Why are you so sure?"

"Because it just can't. The problems of Arabs and Israelis are a bit more complex and multifaceted than the problems of zebras and lions."

"Sometimes complex problems admit of simple answers."

"That may be so, Samuel, but the odds are against it."

"But suppose there was one chance in a hundred that the study of a water hole in Kenya might help bring peace to Jerusalem. Shouldn't you at least look into the matter?"

"Your point is well taken, Samuel. If I could interest some friends of mine in the idea, would you be willing to come to Jerusalem to explain your water hole rules? You always told me you wanted to see the holy places. Well, here's your chance."

"I'm not good with words, Sergio. Others would do a better job at presenting than me. Father Albert from Woomba would be good. If you wish, I'll call him."

"I don't want this Father Albert to do it. I want you."

"Sergio, please. I can't do it. I'd be too nervous. I might start to stutter."

"Say yes, Samuel."

"I'm just a simple man who needs to stand on a stool so that people can see me."

"I don't care about that. Say yes."

"I hope I won't embarrass you too much."

"Is that a yes, Samuel?"

"I guess it is."

"Excuse me a moment." Bonti got up from the table. "Let me make a phone call to the Holy Land."

Sergio Bonti returned in five minutes.

"Would you be ready to fly to Jerusalem in, say, eight hours?"

"Yes."

"Good. I'll pick you up at the Domus in my car, and we'll drive out to Leonardo da Vinci Airport. A private jet will be waiting to take us to Jerusalem."

* * * * * *

As Bishop Harbinger folded the final items to pack for the trip to Jerusalem, the phone rang in his room.

"Bishop Harbinger. This is Giovanni from the switchboard. There's a Sergio Bonti downstairs in the lobby. He says he's here to take you to the airport."

"Tell Signor Bonti I'll be right down."

"Mr. Bonti wants you to bring your pectoral cross and bishop's cassock. Symbols of ecclesiastical authority are important in Palestine."

"I will bring them."

Harbinger put his cassock in his suitcase but couldn't find his pectoral cross.

The phone rang again.

Harbinger hurried down the stairs to the lobby.

"Sorry for the delay, Sergio. I couldn't find my pectoral cross."

Bonti smiled. "You looked everywhere but in the obvious place—it's hanging around your neck."

* * * * * *

Monsignor Remigi knocked at the door of the pope's study.

"Bishop Harbinger is at the airport, Holy Father." The pontiff's secretary blurted out the news.

The pope sat stock still at his desk. "Where is he going? Back to Lipoppo, I assume?"

"No, he's going to Jerusalem."

"Jerusalem! Why?"

"Sergio Bonti, the reporter for *Il Messaggero* is taking him to meet some influential Israelis and Palestinians. The rumor is that he has some ideas for bringing peace to Jerusalem. Whatever these ideas are, Bonti is keeping them under close wraps."

Just then, Cardinal Jensen burst unannounced into the pope's study. He was clearly upset.

"Have you heard? Harbinger is going to Palestine to give a speech. My sources tell me that he will speak on what he calls the rules of the water hole—whatever that means."

Pope Linus fingered his pectoral cross. "I'll almost miss Harbinger. He has certainly animated my schedule over the past several days."

Jensen shook his head. "I think we are all well rid of him."

Chapter Four
Water Hole Rules

The Latin Patriarch of Jerusalem met Bishop Harbinger at the door to the Church of the Holy Sepulcher. Harbinger wept as he knelt before the Tomb of Christ. Reporters and TV camera crews crowded around the bishop as he and the patriarch prayed the rosary. When they had finished, Sergio Bonti led Samuel Harbinger through the narrow streets of Jerusalem to the Wailing Wall, and then up to the Dome of the Rock on the Temple Mount. The visit of the bishop to Jerusalem was being widely covered by the Jewish and Palestinian media. After making all the necessary stops, Harbinger was hosted at a "working lunch" sponsored by Salaam-Shalom, an informal roundtable of Israeli and Palestinian executives. The venue of the luncheon was the King David Hotel.

The main dining room at the hotel was filled to capacity. Those without tickets watched the event on closed-circuit television.

"Three weeks ago," Sergio Bonti began the program, "I sat down next to Samuel Harbinger on a flight from Cairo to Rome.

Neither of us ever imagined that because of that flight, we'd be sitting here today in Jerusalem trying to bring peace to this war-torn city. But in Jerusalem, the unexpected does happen and here we are. So without further ado, let me introduce my friend and fellow traveler, Samuel Harbinger, who will share with us what he calls the rules of the water hole."

Bonti sat down.

"Thank you, Sergio." A waiter brought a Jerusalem phone directory for Harbinger to stand on. "I agree with Sergio. Neither of us ever expected, or indeed ever imagined, that our chance meeting on Egypt Air Flight 850 would lead us here today."

Harbinger paused a moment.

"At the outset, let me say that if you were to come to my village of Lipoppo, you would see a sight that would likely astonish you—elephants, lions, zebras, impalas, and giraffes all using the same water hole. At first, I did not understand how a zebra would come to the water hole and his natural enemy the lion would come as well. Then I began to see that the animals—predator, prey, and scavenger—had developed a series of rules or strategies that allowed them to coexist peaceably at the water hole while still remaining enemies. Let me list some of these rules.

"Rule One. The water hole is a shared space. All animals, whether they are lions, zebras, hippos, elephants, whatever, are welcome to drink there.

"Rule Two. To minimize conflicts, natural enemies will come to the water hole at different times of the day. Zebras, for example, will come to the water hole to drink in the morning; lions will come to drink at night.

"Rule Three. To minimize conflicts further still, natural enemies who come to the water hole at the same time of day will drink in different areas of the water hole. For example, hippos and giraffes both come during the day, but hippos stay in the deep water and giraffes in the shallow water.

"Rule Four. Animals form alliances for their mutual benefit. Because of their height, for example, giraffes can give herd animals early notice of the approach of predators. Herd animals reciprocate. Giraffes must assume awkward positions in order to drink. Herd animals will warn giraffes of predators when they are in these vulnerable positions.

"Rule Five. Herd animals such as zebras, gazelles, and wildebeest often drink close to one another so they can share 'babysitting' responsibilities. For example, zebras and wildebeest assign members of their herd to keep the young from wandering off and getting lost.

"Rule Six. Rogues that do not abide by the rules of the water hole are consequently driven off.

"In keeping Jerusalem peaceful and orderly, Jews and Palestinians could learn much from the simple patterns and habits of life at the water hole."

A shaggy-looking man with sunburned face and tousled hair jumped up and interrupted Bishop Harbinger. Arrogant and boastful, Duke Rayner, Middle East correspondent for *The New York Times*, was generally disliked by members of the press corps. No one, however, would dispute Rayner's professionalism. He always got there first—whether it was a story to be told, or an interview to be had.

"Bishop Harbinger, you don't seriously think that the behavior of animals at a water-fall in Kenya can serve as a model for keeping peace between Jews and Palestinians in Jerusalem?"

"Who is this person you call 'Bishop Harbinger'? I will respond to your question, sir, only if you call me by my real name. My parents did not name me Bishop Harbinger or Your Excellency. They chose to call me Samuel Harbinger."

Several in the audience tittered.

With an arched look, Rayner laughed. "Well, Samuel Harbinger, let me ask you the same question I asked Bishop Harbinger. Do you seriously believe that the behavior of zebras and lions at a water-fall can help in the quest for peace in Jerusalem?"

"Yes, Mr. Rayner, with one important amendment."

"What is that amendment? And please feel free to call me Duke."

"Well, Duke, I said that it was the behavior of animals at the water hole that could help in the quest for peace in Jerusalem. I do not know about animal behavior at a water-fall."

Rayner smiled condescendingly. "I apologize for the mistake, Samuel, but my question goes to the fundamental issue of whether animal behavior can serve as a model for peace in Jerusalem. You believe it can, don't you?"

"Yes, Mr. Rayner, I do."

"This is absurd. It's like running the Roman Empire by reading Aesop's Fables. I'm going to excuse myself."

Sergio Bonti stood up from the table. "Duke, your newspaper has a reputation for open-mindedness. Play the agnostic until you hear Samuel out."

Rayner waved his hand dismissively. "Sergio, after all the decades of bloodshed, you seem to think that the conduct of zebras and lions can contribute to the peace process? With all due respect, that's just downright silly." Rayner gathered his notes and prepared to walk out of the press conference.

Harbinger stared at Rayner. "God created the animals before he created Adam and Eve. Don't be so sure that we can't learn from them. Please sit down, Mr. Rayner and hear me out."

The ballroom fell silent. Rayner glared at Harbinger but sat down. "You've got ten minutes." That's all Rayner said.

"Predators and their prey all need the water hole to survive. Likewise, Jews and Palestinians need Jerusalem for their survival and livelihood. As I mentioned before, the animals work out rules that dictate when they come to the water hole, where they stand, how long they stay. People in Jerusalem must sit down across from one another and negotiate similar rules."

Struck by the utter simplicity of Harbinger's presentation, an Israeli industrialist jumped up from his chair, inadvertently knocking a pitcher of ice water into his wife's lap. Embarrassed by his clumsiness, the man still managed to shout out his question.

"Do you really think that these forms of 'adaptive behavior' could allow the Jews and Palestinians to live in peace in Jerusalem?"

"I do not understand the words 'adaptive behavior.'"

"That's what a Harvard professor would call your water hole rules."

"Then I would answer your question 'yes.' Water hole rules, as I call them, could be worked out between Jews and Palestinians. The key to all of this, of course, depends on finding the person who has the ability to fashion these rules."

"What qualifications should such a person have?" A reporter from the *Jerusalem Post* directed his question to Bishop Harbinger.

Sergio Bonti pushed back his chair and stood. "Samuel, let me try and answer that. Any student of history knows that Jerusalem is a unique place—a city that is holy to three religions. When we leave the King David Hotel after lunch today, we will walk out into a city where Jews, Christians, and Muslims have lived and worshipped for hundreds, and in some cases, for thousands of years. Any successful negotiator must take this reality into account."

"Sergio." A reporter from the Paris daily *Le Figaro* stood up from his seat. "Do you think this person needs to be a Middle East expert?"

"No, on the contrary. I'd rather have a new face with a fresh perspective on the issues."

"What other qualifications should this negotiator have?" The reporter from *Le Figaro* continued questioning Bonti.

"Courage and a willingness to take risks would be high on my list."

"I think you have someone in mind, Bonti. Stop playing cat and mouse with us. Give us the name."

"My distinguished colleague from *Le Figaro* is right. I do have someone in mind."

"Who is it, Sergio?"

With their notepads open, the press corps waited to copy down the name.

"Pope Linus II."

Bonti's suggestion of the Holy Father as the negotiator stunned the audience. No one moved, no one spoke.

Finally, Duke Rayner slammed his hands on the table. "Bonti, just because the pope's gotten all this publicity for dancing in St. Peter's doesn't make him a good choice for this job."

"I know that, Duke. But get by the irrelevant stuff and look carefully at his credentials. The Holy Father has the necessary religious sensitivity, he is not a Middle East expert, and he is courageous and a risk-taker."

"How do we know that the pope is a risk-taker?" Rayner asked.

"He showed his willingness to take risks years ago in Bilbao."

Rayner looked puzzled. "What do you mean 'years ago in Bilbao'?"

"Many of you in this room are too young to remember an incident that occurred when Pope Linus was Archbishop of Bilbao. He walked unannounced into city hall during a hostage crisis and persuaded Basque terrorists to release the mayor and several city councilors. His reward for successfully negotiating the compromise was a bullet in his chest. Someone tried to assassinate him."

The reporter for *The Guardian* asked the key question. "Bishop Harbinger, would you be willing to work with the pope in seeing this initiative through? Pope Linus may have the negotiating skills, but you have an understanding of how these water hole rules work."

Harbinger nodded. "I will do whatever Pope Linus asks of me."

Reporters hurried to fax machines in the King David Hotel. They knew their editors were eagerly awaiting their dispatches.

* * * * * *

The reaction to Bishop Harbinger's remarks at the King David Hotel was sensational to say the least. Newspaper headlines vied with one another in humor. The *Los Angeles Times* was perhaps the most creative. A front-page cartoon showed a lion, a zebra, an elephant, and a hippo lounging around a water hole under the caption, "Drinking Buddies." In a rush to print the paper, the early edition had also included a tiger in the cartoon. The tiger was dropped when a reporter reminded everyone that tigers did not live in Africa, and therefore, could not be "drinking buddies" with lions or zebras.

The Vatican newspaper *L'Osservatore Romano*, however, did not mention or even allude to the Bishop of Lipoppo's luncheon remarks at the King David Hotel in Jerusalem. Reliable sources inside the Vatican reported that Pope Linus, while flattered at being considered for the job, was opposed to becoming involved in what many thought an insoluble situation One Vatican hand summed up the situation this way, "The pope may be infallible on some matters, but Jerusalem isn't one of them." Despite the pope's obvious reluctance to become involved, pressure began to build on Pope Linus to undertake an initiative.

* * * * * *

The private jet carrying Samuel Harbinger set down at a remote hangar at Leonardo da Vinci Airport at 11:35 PM. Ignatius Cropsy waited impatiently until his friend disembarked.

"Well, Samuel, you certainly have caught the attention of the world. You even made it to the cover of *Time* magazine. If you keep up the good work, maybe you'll be chosen Man of the Year."

"I understand the Holy Father wants to see me immediately."

"Yes. He sent me with a car and driver. He was pretty blunt. 'Cropsy, get Harbinger here as soon as possible. No detours.'"

"I guess he's angry because his name was put forward as someone who might be able to settle the Jerusalem question."

"Angry isn't the word I would use. Furious would be more accurate. He even asked Mabibin to do some research on whether a pope has ever had a priest publicly flogged."

"You're joking about Mabibin, aren't you, Ignatius?"

"Of course, I am. But the pope did let loose a couple of well-chosen expletives."

"What's an expletive?"

"It's a word that you wouldn't expect a priest to use, let alone a pope. But he has calmed down a bit."

"Why?"

"After the luncheon, the Executive Committee of Salaam-Shalom met behind closed doors and endorsed the idea of a water hole initiative. From what I understand, the executive committee was impressed by your presentation. One member of the committee went so far as to say he was bowled over by it."

"What did Salaam-Shalom ask the pope and me to do, Cropsy?"

"They wanted you both to approach relevant parties and start a process aimed at bringing peace to Jerusalem. If you would agree to do it, the chairperson of Salaam-Shalom stated that the organization will not only nominate the both of you jointly for the Nobel Peace Prize, it would actively campaign on your behalf."

"I have heard of this prize. Nelson Mandela received it, didn't he?"

"Yes, he did. Let's put it this way, Samuel. Being awarded the Nobel Peace Prize is like being canonized a saint, and you know you can't do much better than that. The possibility of winning the prize for the Catholic Church has to affect the pope's thinking on whether to undertake the initiative."

The car carrying Cropsy and Harbinger pulled up to the back gate of the Vatican. The priests alighted from the car and walked toward the rear entrance of the Apostolic Palace. Swiss Guards snapped to attention as the two men entered the building and climbed up the stairs to the pope's quarters.

Harbinger knocked on the door to the pope's study.

"Come in." The pope sounded tired, thought Harbinger. Crossing himself, Harbinger took a deep breath and pushed open the door.

"Good luck, Samuel," Father Cropsy whispered to his friend as he disappeared into the pope's study.

Chapter Five
A Dog Named Fides

The pontiff sat behind his desk scanning dispatches from nuncios throughout the world.

"Thank you for coming directly from the airport, Bishop Harbinger. I sent Father Ignatius to help get you through security. I understand Father Cropsy is a friend."

"Yes, he met me at the airport when I first arrived in Rome, and since then he has helped me learn to navigate the city."

There was a gentle tap at the door.

"I asked Sister Consuela to fix you a light supper just in case you were hungry."

Sister Consuela entered the room and laid out a basket containing toast with jam and clotted cream. Next to the basket, she placed a large bowl of strawberries. A pot of brewed coffee sat on the pope's desk.

"Thank you, Sister. That will be all. Please close the drapes on your way out."

When Sister Consuela had left, Pope Linus stood up and started to walk around his study..

"Bishop Harbinger, do you know why I had you brought here at this time of night?"

"Yes, Your Holiness. You wished to talk to me about the luncheon at the King David Hotel."

"Yes. Don't you think, my good bishop, that you should have asked me before my name became associated with this new initiative of yours. And don't tell me it was the inspiration of the Holy Spirit that was behind this. He would know better."

"Holy Father, Sergio Bonti proposed your name as someone who has the skill to carry out the water hole initiative. When Bonti brought up what you did in Bilbao, you became the obvious choice."

"How can you compare Bilbao with Jerusalem? I grew up in Basque country, spoke the language, and understood the issues at stake in the hostage crisis. Jerusalem is altogether different. I speak neither Hebrew nor Arabic. I have never lived in Palestine nor have I studied the social dynamics of the place. I wouldn't know a member of Hamas from a member of Hezbollah."

"Holy Father, many in Jerusalem think it doesn't matter whether you speak Hebrew or Arabic or whether you ever lived in Palestine. The problem of Jerusalem will not be solved by professional diplomats with impressive resumes but by men with courage, trustworthiness, and common sense—men like you."

"Explain these water hole rules to me, Bishop Harbinger."

"They are quite simple, Holiness. The water hole provides animals with clean water to drink. If predators like lions and cheetahs killed their prey at the water hole, it would soon become polluted with rotting carcasses. The animals would have to go elsewhere for clean drinking water. So it is in the best interests of all the animals to keep killing to a minimum at the water hole. Instinctively, the animals work out a series of rules to achieve that goal. Predators, for example, come to drink at one time, their prey at another time. Arabs and Jews can develop similar rules aimed at reducing the likelihood of fighting in Jerusalem. When people shop, where people play, which roads people take, when people go to work, when people worship—all these issues can be regulated by what I call water hole rules."

"I understand this organization Salaam-Shalom plans to nominate us for the Nobel Peace Prize if we undertake the initiative."

"Yes, Holiness, that is what I have been told."

The pope walked over to a painting of Saint Peter hanging on the wall. "This man is a hard act to follow. It would be a great honor if the Nobel Peace Prize were awarded to the Catholic Church."

"Yes, it would be."

"If I agree to undertake the initiative, I will wish the first round of negotiations to be in Lipoppo. We can all see firsthand how these water hole rules operate."

"Holiness, you would be most welcome."

"Thank you for all your work on this. I will have an answer soon. But in the meantime, do not speak of your water hole initiative in public."

"Yes, Holy Father."

"Before you go, Bishop Harbinger, I have another matter to discuss with you."

"What is it, Holy Father?"

"You have always advocated my having a dog. I have decided to take your advice."

"That's wonderful news, Holy Father. What convinced you to do it?"

"It was your remark that started me thinking about getting a dog."

"What remark, Holy Father?"

"Your comment that getting a dog would be cheaper than paying for a new conclave to elect my successor. At first I took the comment as impudence, but the more I thought about it, the more I had to agree."

"I did not speak out of impudence, Holy Father. I spoke out of genuine concern for your health."

"It took me time to realize that. But it was the night in St. Peter's Basilica that finally convinced me to get a dog. To see the relationship between the blind man and his corgi service dog was powerful. I asked Paolo Remigi to make a discreet inquiry through our nuncio in London about corgis. The English royal family raises them. When the queen heard of the inquiry, she broke protocol and called me directly."

"Was she helpful?"

"Enormously! I told her I needed a dog that was loyal, a dog that was smart, and a dog that wouldn't be afraid of crowds. The queen gave the corgi an A rating on each of my three points. She does have experience with corgis. She reminded me that at the moment she had thirteen corgis herself."

"Did she mention any negatives?"

"Only one. Corgis are quite sensitive and do not take well to criticism. The queen put it this way, 'If you punish a corgi, there will be some form of retaliation, rest assured of that.' She then offered me my choice of her latest litter. Paolo flew to London and chose a black and white male."

"When will the corgi arrive, Holy Father?"

"Next week, but *L'Osservatore Romano* will run a story today. There should be some time for people to adjust to the idea of a dog at the Vatican. There will be some grumbling but nothing too serious."

"Who will object?"

"For sure, Jensen will. You know how he is with animals. But I'm ready to counter his arguments. I'm actually curious to see what arguments he makes."

"What do you mean, Holy Father?"

"Jensen knows his theology. He won't argue that animals do not have souls. Pope John Paul II determined that animals were part of God's creation and in fact had souls. If Jensen argues that popes have traditionally not kept pets, Remigi has a list of popes who have had them. For example, Benedict XV had a dog, Pius XI kept an eagle, Pius XII had canaries, and a goldfish named Gretchen. Many other popes have had cats. Back in the sixteenth century, Leo X even kept an elephant. Jensen's strongest objection is the health issue. Some employees will either be afraid of a dog or a cat or have some sort of allergic reaction to animals. But if service animals are routinely allowed in the Vatican, one more animal should not create an undue burden on Vatican resources."

"What will you name him?"

"Political realities being what they are, I'm going to have to give him a Latin name. If I choose an English name, the Russians will object. If I choose an Italian name, the Spanish will object. If I choose a Basque name, the Finns will probably object."

"What name have you chosen?"

"I narrowed the list down to three: *Fides*—Faith, *Spes*—Hope, and *Caritas*—Charity. I chose *Fides*."

"A good choice, Holiness."

* * * * * *

As expected, Cardinal Jensen gave an interview to a reporter from *L'Osservatore Romano* to discuss the corgi given to the pope by the the queen of England. Jensen pointed out that the queen, not the archbishop of Canterbury, was the head of the Church of England. Therefore, when one head of religion, in this case the queen, gives something of value to another head of religion, in this case the pope, theologians should carefully scrutinize the transaction to make sure that the gift is secular, not religious in nature. "Given the historical tensions between the the Roman Catholic Church and the Church of England ," Jensen noted, "a high level of scrutiny is called for."

Pope Linus smiled when he read the interview. "I didn't expect a theological objection from Jensen. He always does the unexpected."

* * * * * *

From the moment Fides set foot in the Vatican, he was an instant celebrity. Under a headline called "Corgimania," *Il Messaggero* cataloged Fides' activities during his first week "in office."

On day one, Fides broke free from Sister Consuela and raced across St. Peter's Square with a contingent of Swiss Guards in hot pursuit. Fides was finally cornered in a religious article store after toppling over display cabinets full of what one newspaper dubbed "paraphernalia for the pious."

On day two, Fides again broke free from Sister Consuela. He was found drinking out of a holy water fount just inside the door of the basilica. Rome's sanitation authorities investigated but found no violation of city health codes.

On day three, a group of children from Rome brought their pets to St. Peter's Square on the off chance that Fides might play with them. The play date ended rather abruptly when a boa constrictor wrapped itself around Fides in a potentially fatal hug.

Day four turned into an international incident. Fides escaped from the papal apartment and went on an unaccompanied tour of the Sistine Chapel and the Borgia Apartments with their collection of Raphael frescoes. When word of what happened leaked out, art historians were appalled. Overnight, an ad hoc committee formed and several members of the group flew to Rome to express their "gravest concern" over Fides' conduct. The Italian minister of tourism also visited the Vatican to emphasize the Italian government's concern about the matter.

Day five saw a lost Fides that resulted in a top to bottom search of the Apostolic Palace. Fides was finally found in the Vatican kitchen sampling various dishes. Gnocchi and tiramisu seemed to be his favorites.

On day six, Fides was driven out to Castel Gandolfo—the papal summer palace.

On day seven, Fides rested.

Since pictures of Fides commanded high prices, paparazzi prowled the Vatican looking for any sign of the papal corgi. In the tourist shops that clustered around St. Peter's Square, vendors sold Fides' postcards by the thousands. Some were captioned *Il Cane Santo*—roughly translated the Holy Dog. Others showed the pope throwing a ball to Fides in the Vatican Gardens. The most expensive card showed the queen and Pope Linus with Fides standing between them. The Vatican post office was swamped by deliveries of canine clothing, from blankets to boots to leashes. There was even some preliminary talk of issuing a commemorative stamp in honor of Fides.

* * * * * *

Pope Linus II loved every minute of life in his post-corgi world, at least until the encyclical incident. On this particular night, Pope Linus took Fides for a late walk in the Vatican Gardens. A stray cat caught Fides' attention. Barking loudly, the dog went off in hot pursui of the stray. Fides was gone for twenty minutes. Angry at the dog's disappearance, Pope Linus forgot the queen's caveat about chastening a corgi. Not only did the pontiff raise his voice to Fides, he did not give the dog his customary after-walk biscuit.

That night, Pope Linus worked late on a preliminary draft of a papal encyclical entitled in Latin *Ecclesia Universalis*—the Universal Church. As with other popes before him, Linus used encyclicals to communicate his views on issues facing the church. When he awoke, he turned on the light. Strewn across the floor was the text of the encyclical.

Fides sat on the end of the bed grooming his fur as it nothing had happened. Pope Linus remembered too late the queen's remark. If you punish a corgi, he will retaliate.

Ecclesia Universalis was ultimately published. Among Vatican insiders, some of the more dubious points of reasoning were often attributed to Fides. One prelate would say humorously that the encyclical contained more bark than bite.

Chapter Six
Plastic Furniture

Rumors spread that the pope would use his homily at Sunday Mass on February 22, the Feast of the Chair of Saint Peter the Apostle, to respond to Salaam-Shalom's petition to undertake the Jerusalem initiative.

On that day, a sign outside the front entrance to St. Peter's Basilica announced in Italian and in English that seating for today's 10:00 AM papal Mass would be limited. Despite the uncertainty of gaining admittance, by 6:00 AM, a long line of people had gathered outside the cathedral. The possibility of witnessing a historic moment in the Middle East peace process was enough to entice many Romans to come to St. Peter's Square so early in the morning.

At 7:00 AM, the television networks arrived. Under the watchful eyes of uniformed Swiss Guards, camera crews began unloading equipment from their trucks and vans.

A moment of humor was injected into the scene when a Swiss

Guard chased a disheveled-looking man carrying a sign, "Enough Already" out of the square.

Punctually at 9:45 AM, Pope Linus walked from the Apostolic Palace to St. Peter's Basilica. When he reached the entrance door, he stopped a moment until the choir intoned the papal hymn *Tu es Petrus*—"You are Peter and upon this rock I will build my church." Preceded by several concelebrants, the pontiff walked down the nave of the church responding to applause from the crowds. There was a feeling of electricity in the air as the pope genuflected at the foot of the high altar and climbed slowly up the steps to the papal throne. Before sitting down, he turned to the congregation and raised his hand in blessing. The crowd erupted with wild cheers and applause. Reporters strained to see who was on the altar with the pope. The press was especially eager to learn the whereabouts of Bishop Harbinger. There was a story making the rounds that if Bishop Harbinger were in the procession, the initiative would be a "go." If he wasn't, the initiative was dead. In that case, the Vatican would most likely issue a statement in "Pope Speak"—a language once described by an old Vatican hand as a mix of five percent euphemism, ten percent elision, twenty percent ellipsis, thirty percent euphony, and one hundred percent obfuscation.

The statement in "Pope Speak" would read something like, "The Bishop of Lipoppo and I are, of course, deeply grieved by the loss of life in the Middle East. God has given life; it is not for man to take it away, whether it is through capital punishment, abortion, or acts of terrorism. Conscious of the many people and organizations who have asked the bishop and me to intervene in the Middle East conflict; I have asked Cardinal Whomever to fly to Jerusalem to assess the chances for a broad and lasting peace. Cardinal Whomever knows full well that such a peace must rest on justice and fairness for all parties."

When the Bishop of Lipoppo was not seen on the altar, some reporters started writing their "Cardinal Whomever" dispatches.

When the cheering ended, the pope began saying Mass.

During a choral interlude before the reading of the Gospel, the pope's secretary, Monsignor Paolo Remigi, walked over to the Holy Father and whispered in his ear. The pope nodded; a hint of a smile crossed his face.

After the newly appointed Archbishop of Quito, Ecuador, read the Gospel, the pope rose from his throne and stood on the top step of the altar. Cardinal Sebastiano Bagonninni, the Vatican secretary of state and number two man in the church hierarchy, handed Pope Linus a prepared text. Warm and approachable with an almost boyish grin, Roman-born Bagonninni would have been considered a possible successor to Pope Linus but for his age (almost seventy-five), his health (Addison's disease), and his name (too unpronounceable). When he was named to the number two position in the Vatican, the good-natured Bagonninni asked Pope Linus whether the Holy Father wanted someone with four n's in his name representing the Catholic Church worldwide. The pope is said to have smiled at his secretary of state. "Your Eminence, I might wish to revisit the issue if you add a fifth 'n' to your name but not before."

Pope Linus put on his glasses. "Today the Holy City of Jerusalem is a city that is at war with itself. Jew fights Muslim, and Muslim fights Jew."

Old Vatican hands looked surprised. The pope was speaking in English—a language he rarely used. A reporter from the *Herald Tribune* chuckled. "He wants no one to misinterpret what he says—especially no one in the press corps. Most of us do better understanding his heavily accented English than his flawless Latin or Basque."

"The last decades," said the pope in measured tones, "have seen renewed efforts to bring peace to the Holy Land. All of these efforts have failed. Now I have been asked by many individuals and organizations to undertake an initiative aimed at bringing peace to Jerusalem. Because of a speech by the bishop of Lipoppo at the King David Hotel in the Holy City, the press has labeled the effort as the water hole initiative. Many see in the bishop's simple wisdom a way to help bring peace to Jerusalem."

Putting aside his prepared text, the pope paused a moment adding to the suspense of what he would say.

"I have spoken to the Israeli government and the Palestine Liberation Organization and have agreed to undertake such an initiative if two conditions are met. First, only one representative from each side can participate in the discussions—at least initially. Second, the discussions must take place in the village of Lipoppo in Kenya. Where better place than that for all the parties to observe the rules of the water hole. My secretary, Monsignor Remigi, has just now informed me that both Israel and the Palestine Liberation Organization have agreed to my conditions. Each government has designated its foreign minister as its representative. I should also add my thanks to the government of Kenya for its enthusiastic support of the peace initiative. Therefore, on this propitious day, a day dedicated to the Chair of Saint Peter the Apostle, I formally invite the foreign ministers of Israel and the Palestine Liberation Organization to come to Lipoppo on March seventh to begin the peace process. In anticipation of the agreement by both sides, I asked Bishop Harbinger to return to Lipoppo yesterday to begin making the necessary arrangements for the meeting. May God bless our efforts."

When Pope Linus had finished his remarks, Cardinal Bagonninni slipped off the altar and hurried to his office. Cardinal Jensen stopped him in the corridor.

"Sebastiano, the pope has lost his judgment – first the dog and now this."

"Take these matters up with the Holy Father, Martin, not with me."

Several of Bagonninni's staff stood nervously outside his office. Bagonninni smiled. "It's a 'go.' Fax the pontiff's invitation to the foreign minister of Israel and the foreign minister of the Palestine Liberation Organization. Copies of the invitation should be sent to all heads of state."

Bagonninni handed a letter to one of his assistants. "This goes to Bishop Harbinger in Lipoppo."

* * * * * *

The postman Obani hurried to the rectory.

"This letter has just come, Bishop Samuel. It looks like it is from the pope. It came over the banker's machine—the one that needs no postman for delivery."

Samuel Harbinger smiled. "You mean it came over the banker's fax machine."

"Yes, the fax machine—the machine that needs no postman for delivery." Obani never let an opportunity go by without expressing concern about this machine in the banker's office.

Harbinger looked at the name of the sender. It was Cardinal Sebastiano Bagonninni, the Vatican secretary of state.

"No, it is not from the pope but from Cardinal Bagonninni. He is in charge of the Vatican's relations with countries throughout the world."

"Must you leave us again, Bishop? The last time a letter came from Rome, you left us for a month. The confirmation of Edith's son and daughter has already been scheduled for next week and two weddings the week after. I have delivered all the invitations."

"Obani, let's see first what Cardinal Bagonninni says."

Harbinger took the letter and began to read the contents aloud. Thank God, he thought, the letter was in English not in Latin.

Vatican City, February 22

Greetings to His Excellency Samuel Harbinger
Bishop of the Diocese of Lipoppo, Kenya

His Holiness Pope Linus II will make a fraternal visit to the Diocese of Lipoppo between March 7 and March 9. The foreign ministers of Israel and the Palestine Liberation Organization will accompany him.

Several issues should be mentioned in passing. First, Your Excellency will arrange for air transportation for the Holy Father from Rome to Lipoppo. Second, the Holy Father and his guests are coming to Lipoppo to observe a water hole in the vicinity of the village. Pope Linus asks you therefore to provide dignified amenities consistent with this purpose. Third, the Holy Father will celebrate a Pontifical High Mass in Lipoppo on the night of March 8. To help plan for this Mass and coordinate other matters concerning the pope's visit, I am dispatching to Lipoppo, Father Ignatius Cropsy, whom I understand is known to you.

Yours in Christ,
Cardinal Sebastiano Bagonninni
Vatican Secretary of State

P.S.   His Holiness will bring Fides, his pet corgi, with him.

* * * * * *

That night, Bishop Harbinger called the village together.

"The Holy Father is coming to pay us a visit. He will say a Pontifical High Mass on the night of March eighth."

"What do we need for such a Mass, Bishop Harbinger?" Agatha, the village dressmaker, always asked the hard questions.

Harbinger shrugged. "Father Cropsy will know what is required. We will ask him when he arrives. The letter also mentions the water hole. The pope and his two friends will want to see it."

"Why does the pope wish to see the water hole?" Agatha asked her second question. "Will he take pictures of the animals?"

Bishop Harbinger smiled. "The pope is not here on safari, Agatha. He wishes to learn how the animals react to one another when they come to the water hole."

"We all know that."

"But the pope and his friends do not."

Agatha stared at Bishop Harbinger with a baffled look. "If the pope is so important a person, how can he not know about the rules of the water hole?"

"He lives far away in Rome. They have things there called water fountains but no water holes. We must help him learn those rules. Perhaps when he understands them, he can bring peace to Jerusalem."

Obani's face lit up. "I've heard of Jerusalem. Jesus was born there many years ago. It must be a holy city."

Harbinger smiled at Obani. "You must start reading the New Testament again, Obani. Jesus was born in Bethlehem. He was crucified in Jerusalem."

"Does it matter if I have the places wrong? We are Christians because Jesus died for us. We are not Christians because Jesus died for us in Jerusalem."

Harbinger stared at the postman of Lipoppo. "You are right, Obani."

* * * * * *

After two days of briefing by officials of the Vatican Secretariat of State, Father Ignatius Cropsy boarded an Egypt Air flight to Nairobi. John Palestro, a Dominican monk and old friend from seminary days, met Cropsy at the airport. After Cropsy had freshened up, the two priests went out to dinner at a restaurant frequented by Nairobi's expat community.

"By the way, John, you promised to get me on a flight to Lipoppo. I should leave tomorrow. Bishop Harbinger needs my help to prepare for the pope's arrival."

"Don't worry, you're all booked."

"On what airline, John?"

"It's not exactly an airline. You're flying with Slocum in his two-seat Piper Cub."

"What do you mean?"

"Slocum is the best bush pilot in Nairobi. If you want to get to Lipoppo, go with him. I have you scheduled to leave tomorrow morning."

"You say he's the best pilot around?"

"Absolutely. Do you see that guy sitting at the bar?"

"The one who just staggered in from the washroom?"

"Yes. That's Slocum."

"He's pretty drunk. How is he going to be sober enough to get the plane off the ground?"

"Don't ask me, but he always does. He has drafted an 'extenuating circumstances' clause in his contract that allows him to cancel for all sorts of reasons including liquor. But to my knowledge he has never relied on it to get out of a contract."

"What time do we leave?"

"Slocum told me ten AM. But he's lived in Kenya long enough to be 'Africanized.' When he quotes a departure time of ten o'clock, he is giving a range—he could leave as early as eight AM or as late as noon. He'll call your hotel when he's ready to go."

"What's Slocum's full name?"

"No one knows. He's just Slocum to the expat community. One more thing, Ignatius. Slocum's plane is a bit ramshackle. It may bump around a bit as it lands. Not to worry. Slocum has never lost a passenger."

* * * * * *

Ignatius Cropsy looked out the left side of the Piper Cub. He saw the water hole in the distance—a blue smudge on the brown landscape of East Africa. Every now and then, the sun would flash on the water reminding Cropsy of his mother's sapphire ring. As a child, he would sometimes rummage through his mother's jewelry box and take out the ring. He was fascinated how the stone would sparkle and toss light off in every direction.

Slocum interrupted Cropsy's reveries. "Okay, Father. It's time to land this leaky oil bucket. Let's find a place that looks flat."

"Where do you usually land, Slocum?"

"Usually land?" Slocum smiled. "I've never landed at Lipoppo before. But it looks doable."

Father Cropsy, always nervous during take-offs and landings, turned the color of an altar cloth. "You've never landed here before?"

"Never, Father. In fact, I don't think anyone has ever landed here before."

"Then why didn't we come to Lipoppo by car or truck?"

"Blame that cheerful friend of yours."

"Bishop Samuel?"

"Yes. He persuaded me to fly in. He's always so happy and upbeat. It's hard saying no to him."

"But there's no runway here."

"Samuel promised he'd clear a flat space so we could land."

"Where is it, Slocum?"

The pilot squinted into the sun. "If I had to guess, I'd say it's that open space near where those people are standing. It looks pretty flat to me."

"Who are the people?"

"It looks like a welcoming committee. At least I'm going to act on that assumption. There's not much fuel left." Slocum aimed his Piper Cub at the open space.

"Hold on, Father, the landing's going to be a bit bumpy."

"I feel ill."

"There's no time for that now. Just hold on."

As the plane's wheels were seconds away from touching the ground, a cape buffalo ran out onto the makeshift runway.

"Damn it. We have to go up again, Father, or we'll have a dead cape buffalo on our hands. That wouldn't be the best way for you to arrive in Africa."

Slocum pulled up the nose of the plane and with full throttle, began climbing. The wheels of the Piper Cub almost touched the animal's horns. Slocum turned the plane around and made another approach. He shook his head in disbelief. "That buffalo isn't moving. I'll have to land in that field over there."

His face still pale from nausea, Father Cropsy held tightly to his seat belt.

"Here we go, Father. Pray that there aren't any boulders in the field."

The plane bounced its way along the ground and skidded to a halt.

Slocum pushed open the cockpit and helped a rather wobbly Cropsy climb down to the ground. Bishop Harbinger ran up and hugged his friend.

"Welcome to Lipoppo, Ignatius. I'm sorry about the buffalo. There must be a reason why he didn't want you to land on our makeshift runway."

When Father Ignatius Cropsy had agreed to come to Lipoppo to help coordinate the pope's visit, he didn't realize that the assignment would entail landing in places where the term "runway" would not only be overly generous, it would be outright misleading.

"The cape buffalo was right." Slocum had walked over to inspect the runway that the village had prepared. "Look—the ground isn't stable here. If I had landed on the makeshift runway, the weight of the plane would have opened a sinkhole the size of a house."

Bishop Harbinger smiled at his friend. "You have learned your first lesson about Africa, Ignatius. In Genesis, it says that God created the animals before he created man. Animals can be your friends and your teachers."

"Well, Samuel Harbinger, I guess I have lots to learn."

"Lots, Ignatius, but you are a good student. You'll learn fast."

A Range Rover pulled alongside the plane and several villagers transferred Cropsy's luggage into the back of the vehicle.

"We traded in our village Jeep for this Range Rover. Everyone is so proud of it," the bishop said.

After pouring some fuel into the tank of the plane, Slocum shook hands with the two priests.

"I'm off. Lipoppo is not on too many maps, but as of today, it has air access. A couple of suggestions, Bishop Harbinger. First, build Lipoppo something that resembles a runway, and second, implement some animal control measures. No pilot will want to dodge animals as he is trying to get in and out of here."

The bishop nodded. "Yes, we will. Ignatius and I may have more work for you. Here's my calling card—I got it in Rome."

Slocum turned the card in different directions. "It's hard to make out the phone numbers with these pictures on it. Who are they anyway? One looks like a woman and the other a bird sitting on her shoulder."

"It's the Virgin Mary and the Holy Ghost."

"Oh! Let me get you one of mine." Slocum hunted through his trousers' pockets until he pulled out a whiskey-stained piece of paper with his name and phone number. "Call me whenever. For the right price, I'll fly the devil into Lipoppo."

Harbinger had to laugh at Slocum's poor choice of a passenger.

"That won't be necessary, my friend. Father Crosky will be in touch."

"It's Cropsy. Samuel never gets my name right."

The plane took off in a cloud of dust and slowly disappeared into the haze of the midday sky. The two priests walked back toward the village.

"Well, Samuel Harbinger, Bishop of Lipoppo, we have a lot of work ahead of us. It's not easy organizing a papal visit."

"Cardinal Bagonninni's letter says that the pope will say a Pontifical High Mass on March eighth. What does that mean?"

"It's a special Mass said by the pope."

"Aren't all Masses the same?"

"Yes, but if the pope says it ..."

"Is it more of a Mass than if you or I said it?"

"Not exactly."

"What does Lipoppo need to do to have such a Mass?"

"First of all, you need concelebrants."

"Where do you find such things?"

Cropsy smiled. "Concelebrants are priests who say the Mass with the pope. You and I could concelebrate. Are there any other priests in the vicinity?"

"Father Albert lives twenty-five kilometers away in Woomba. He will be a concelebrant."

"Well, the procession would look better if there were five concelebrants. Let me ask Bishop Patti whether we can get by with three."

"You'll have to ask the papal master of ceremonies?"

"Yes, he's the final word on all matters of papal liturgy. Assuming Patti allows three, you'll also need altar servers, tall candlesticks, and incense."

"We have altar servers and at least one tall candlestick. Bagua, my housekeeper, can probably make incense from the sap of a gum tree."

"We'll also need people to swing censers, carry the pope's staff and miter, and receive the Eucharist before the pope does."

"Receive the Eucharist before the pope does? I don't understand."

"In a Pontifical Mass, you have a ceremony called the *praegustatio*. Someone receives a piece of the consecrated bread before the pope does—just in case someone tries to poison him."

"Tries to poison the pope?"

"Yes, in the bad old days, people used to try to kill the pope by poisoning the bread and wine."

"We don't need this *pergustio* or whatever it's called. No one from Lipoppo would try to kill the pope."

"I'm sure we can remove the ritual. I agree it's a bit silly in this day and age. Now onto a more important matter. Do you have a choir?"

"No, but Obani's son will sing at Mass. He used to sing at a night club in Kinshasa."

The vision of a Kenyan heartthrob in tight pants and an open shirt crooning "On Eagle's Wings" to the pope sent chills down Cropsy's spine.

"All things considered, Samuel, I think I will recommend to Bishop Patti that Pope Linus not celebrate a Pontifical High Mass in the village—a regular Mass will do fine."

"And what about children bringing their pets to Mass?"

"No. Pope Linus agrees with Cardinal Jensen that allowing animals in church distracts people from focusing on the liturgy. He is adamant on that. The pope is bringing Fides with him, but he will not be allowed to enter the church."

"Ignatius, sometimes Rome worries too much about guarding the past and not enough about making way for the future."

Harbinger looked again at Cardinal Bagonninni's letter. "The cardinal also mentions providing 'dignified amenities' at the water hole. Ignatius, get in the village Range Rover. Obani will take us out to the water hole so I can show you what I've done already."

Obani drove the Range Rover slowly across the flat savannah, trying without too much success, to avoid potholes. Finally, several trees appeared on the horizon.

Harbinger tugged at Cropsy's arm. "There it is, Ignatius. The water hole should be pretty crowded this time of day—mostly herd animals like gazelles and zebras."

Obani bounced the Range Rover up to a wooden platform that had been built just back from the water's edge.

"I asked Hestern, the village carpenter, to build it for the pope and his guests."

"Good job! What's on the platform, Samuel?"

"Come up and let me show you."

Harbinger scampered up the platform like an excited child in search of his birthday presents. Cropsy climbed up behind him.

"Well, what do you think?"

Arranged in neat clusters were sets of plastic beach furniture—yellow umbrellas and white chairs and tables.

"Mobeki traveled once to Zanzibar and saw people sitting

along the water's edge with chairs and umbrellas like these. I ordered four sets of the plastic furniture from a mail order catalog." Harbinger bubbled with excitement. "Do you think the pope will like them? I got them in yellow and white—the papal colors, but I could get different colors if you think yellow and white would offend the Israelis or the Palestinians."

"I don't think it's the colors that are the problem, Samuel."

"Then what's wrong with them, Cropsy?"

"It's a question of *gravitas*."

"What does *gravitas* mean?"

"It's a Latin word for demeanor—a pope must always look like a pope. Sitting on a plastic chair under a plastic beach umbrella … well, it detracts from his *gravitas*."

"Why?"

"It's hard to explain why—it just does. When we get back to Lipoppo, let me fax Cardinal Bagonninni to be absolutely sure."

"Why Bagonninni and not Patti?"

"This is not a question of liturgy; it's a question of politics. That's Cardinal Bagonninni's domain."

* * * * * *

Cropsy had hardly sent the fax before the secretary of state responded.

"No plastic beach chairs or umbrellas—no matter what their color. They detract from *gravitas* and an image of professionalism that Pope Linus seeks to foster. Replace them with wooden chairs and tables and a thatched roof over the viewing platform."

Samuel Harbinger stood with the despondent look of a child whose parents had just made fun of his choice of Christmas presents.

"Ignatius, what else detracts from Pope Linus' *gravitas*?"

"Hawaiian shirts, Bermuda shorts, skimpy underpants, chewing gum, riding on an elephant, ballroom dancing—things like that."

"What about gingersnaps?"

"Gingersnaps?"

"Yes. I asked my housekeeper, Bagua, to bake a plate of gingersnaps for His Holiness. Her gingersnaps are the best in the village. If he eats them, will they ruin his *gravitas*?"

"Gingersnaps will be okay."

"And what about suntan oil and bug repellant?"

"They're okay as well."

* * * * * *

On the morning of March 2, Duke Rayner, Middle East correspondent for *The New York Times,* drove his Jeep into the village of Lipoppo.

He stopped at the post office and spoke to Obani.

"Where is your pastor, Bishop Harbinger?"

"He is in the church. He is very busy today. The pope is coming to Lipoppo in a few days."

"Show me the church. I promise I won't take up too much of your pastor's time."

Obani pointed to a small building surmounted by a cross.

"There's the church, but remember Bishop Harbinger is very busy. We worry about him. He came to my house last night for dinner but he did not finish his food."

The visitor knocked on the church door.

"Come in. I'll be with you in a minute."

When the reporter pushed open the church door, he saw Bishop Harbinger cleaning the windows with a wet towel attached to a broom handle.

"Do you remember me? I'm Duke Rayner, Middle East correspondent for *The New York Times.* I was the one who almost walked out of your press conference at the King David Hotel."

"Yes, Mr. Rayner, now I remember. I apologize for cutting you off so abruptly."

"I think I'm the one who owes the apology."

"It was nothing. Do you live in New York? My brother Vincent lives there. He owns a nightclub in Harlem. Maybe you've heard of it. It's called The Conclave."

"No, I haven't. New York's a big town."

"Are you here for the papal visit?"

"Yes, I would like to look around Lipoppo to get a feel for the place."

"By all means. I apologize for the plastic beach chairs and umbrellas on the observation deck. They will be removed once wooden chairs and tables are found."

"What's wrong with plastic beach furniture?"

"Cardinal Bagonninni said plastic furniture will detract from Pope Linus' *gravitas* and the image of professionalism that should surround the meeting."

"*Gravitas* and the image of professionalism are big bites for a small village like Lipoppo to digest."

That night Duke Rayner faxed his first dispatch from the village of Lipoppo.

"Pope Linus II will land in Lipoppo in a few days time. For those of you who have seen the Broadway musical *Brigadoon*, Lipoppo will remind you of that mythical, almost mystical Scottish village. Lipoppo is a place where Obani, the postman, stops at everyone's house whether or not he has mail to deliver. It is also a place where Kareri, the village seamstress, will make a child's confirmation outfit in one day and then spend the next two days fitting it perfectly. This is not to say, however, that problems do not arise in Lipoppo but when they do, there is almost a charming simplicity about them. Take the incident of the plastic beach furniture. To provide shade for the pope and the foreign ministers at the water hole, Bishop Harbinger, the village pastor, an uncomplicated man with a winning smile, ordered plastic beach chairs, tables, and umbrellas from a mail order catalog. The Vatican thought the furniture detracted from the image of professionalism that should surround the meeting. The bishop's superiors in Rome told the pastor to replace the plastic beach furniture with a thatched roof and wooden chairs. I don't know how you feel about it, but I vote 'yes' for the plastic beach furniture and 'no' for the thatched roof and wooden chairs."

Rayner's story appeared on the front page of the next day's *The New York Times*. Within minutes after the paper reached the newsstands, the phones in the offices of the Archdiocese of New York started ringing off the hook. One by one, New Yorkers began registering their vote in favor of the plastic beach furniture. One woman became so incensed at the Vatican's attitude that she offered to buy the chairs and umbrellas for $25,000 but only if they were used for the papal visit. Within minutes, another caller had raised the amount to $40,000 whether or not the furniture was used during the papal visit.

A second fax arrived in Lipoppo from Cardinal Bagonninni's office. The message was not written in "Pope Speak."

"Disregard earlier fax—plastic beach furniture okay."

* * * * * *

As the day of the pope's arrival approached, Bishop Harbinger's "must-do" list grew progressively longer until finally it topped out at twenty-eight items. As one might have expected, the issue that generated the most controversy was Pope Linus' travel arrangements—most notably which airline would fly the pontiff from Rome to Lipoppo.

Years before, Alitalia, Italy's national air carrier, and the Vatican had negotiated an informal agreement covering the pope's foreign travel. Under this arrangement, one of Alitalia's commercial fleet—dubbed Shepherd One for the occasion—would take the pope to his foreign destination. For local flights inside the country of destination, the pope would take the national airline of that country. Assuming this agreement was followed in this case, Alitalia would fly the pope from Rome to Nairobi, and Kenya Airways from Nairobi to Lipoppo.

Given the worldwide interest in the pope's trip to Africa,

however, Alitalia pressured the Vatican to renegotiate the agreement to give Alitalia the option of flying the pontiff even on purely domestic legs of his trip. Kenya Airways took issue with Alitalia's proposal, insisting that it be allowed to provide the air service between Nairobi and Lipoppo.

Bishop Harbinger consulted Slocum, the only person to have landed a plane in Lipoppo. Slocum's recommendation carried great weight with Harbinger. Given that both Alitalia and Kenya Airways planned to use small jets to bring the pope to Lipoppo, Slocum advised Harbinger to reject both proposals and let him use his Piper Cub to bring the pope from Nairobi to Lipoppo. He told Harbinger, "The runway in Lipoppo can handle jets but just barely. Given that the pope is the passenger, let's err on the side of caution and not use a jet."

Tempers also flared over the issue of when each party would land in Lipoppo. No one seemed to dispute the Vatican's position that Pope Linus, as host of the meeting, should fly into Lipoppo first. The Israelis, citing "historical reasons," insisted that its minister should fly into Lipoppo second. The Israelis were not particularly forthcoming in explaining what these "historical reasons" were, other than to say that the matter spoke for itself.

The PLO, however, argued that its minister should arrive second "for equitable and geopolitical reasons." As with the Israelis' use of the phrase "historical reasons," the Palestine Liberation Organization did not elaborate on the meaning of its phrase, "for equitable and geopolitical reasons."

The pilot Slocum, however, came up with a practical solution that ignored both the Israeli and Palestinian positions. After he brought the pope to Lipoppo, Slocum would fly to the town of Woomba. In Woomba, he would pick up the Israeli and the Palestine Liberation Organization foreign ministers and then fly them in the same plane back to Lipoppo. Thus, the two ministers would arrive in Lipoppo at precisely the same time. When a reporter reminded Slocum that his Piper Cub seated only one passenger, the pilot said that on several occasions in the past, he had "squeezed in" a second passenger.

Arranging ground accommodations in Lipoppo for the pope and the ministers created its own set of problems. The Council of Elders insisted on allocating housing in the village. They decided to give the pope a room in the church rectory, the Israeli minister a room in the schoolhouse, and the Palestinian minister a room in the post office. The room assignments were hardly finalized before the Council of Elders began receiving complaints.

Father Cropsy pointed out that the pope's room in the rectory had no running water. An advance man for the Palestine Liberation Organization complained that the room in the post office was too noisy. Not only did Obani start sorting the mail at 2:00 AM, a woman from the village began making phone calls at 3:00 AM. The Council of Elders did ask Obani to delay sorting the mail until 4:00 AM. As for the woman phone-caller, the Council of Elders sent a message back to the Palestinians. "The woman making the calls is Zamba's wife. She speaks with her daughter in South Africa several times a day. You try to stop her. We can't."

The Israelis complained that the room in the schoolhouse was too small for the foreign minister and his Mossad agent. When the Israelis were reminded that each party was permitted only one person at the meeting in Lipoppo, they stated that a Mossad agent should not be looked on as a separate person from the minister but as a shadow of the minister. Ignatius Cropsy branded the Israeli argument as sophistry. Showing an uncharacteristic firmness, the Council of Elders refused to change room assignments except that the pope and Bishop Harbinger were allowed to switch rooms in order to give the pope a room with running water. Not surprisingly, the Mossad agent was refused entrance to Lipoppo.

* * * * * *

On the morning of March 7, the villagers of Lipoppo were up long before the sun. They were in a festive mood. Agatha, the dressmaker, had given birth to a healthy boy during the night. The village midwife said it boded well for the pope's visit.

Bishop Harbinger said Mass on the village soccer field at 7:00 AM to accommodate the large number of worshippers who had come from as far away as fifty kilometers to see the pope. When Mass was over, the crowd began to scan the heavens. The flight was due to arrive at 10:00 AM, but everyone knew that times of arrival were not hard and fast guarantees in Kenya.

Although all aspects of the pope's arrival had been carefully planned, Harbinger had one nagging concern. Would the pope's arrival in Slocum's battered Piper Cub detract from papal *gravitas*? He asked Duke Rayner from *The New York Times*.

"Bishop Harbinger, let me assure you of one thing. The picture of Pope Linus landing in the African bush aboard a battered Piper Cub on a mission of world peace will be a public relations triumph. If this were a U.S. presidential election, I'd say the pope was about to get a big boost in the opinion polls."

Chapter Seven
A Pope Visits Lipoppo

"There it is." Bagua, the bishop's housekeeper, saw the plane first.

Harbinger breathed a sigh of relief. At least Slocum had not gotten drunk and exercised the "extenuating circumstances" clause in his contract.

As the plane circled to make its approach, Harbinger's heart beat faster. He had reviewed the details of Pope Linus' arrival with Cropsy only an hour before. Were this not Africa, Harbinger thought to himself, he would have felt more confident that everything would run smoothly. But this was Africa, and Africa was always unpredictable.

As Slocum made his approach to the runway, the engine of his Piper Cub backfired. The noise sounded like the report of a rifle. Frightened, a flock of herons flew up from the water hole, right into the path of the approaching Piper Cub. When he looked out the window, all Slocum could see were white feathers.

"Holy Father, hold on," shouted Slocum. "The herons are

flying up, so to get away from them, I'll have to dive. Say a couple of prayers."

As Slocum approached the runway for the second time, Harbinger could sense that this time Slocum meant business. Neither herons nor water buffalo were going to interfere with this landing. Harbinger made the sign of the cross as the plane hit the ground in a cloud of dust. After bouncing over the uneven ground for six hundred meters or more, one of the tires blew out. The plane collapsed on the ground like an exhausted winged dinosaur.

Slocum pushed open the cockpit window and held up two fingers in a victory salute. "Shepherd One reporting. We have landed successfully in Lipoppo. They'll be a twenty-minute layover here while I change a tire. Then it'll be off to Woomba."

After taking off his goggles and earphone, Slocum jumped to the ground and helped the much-relieved Pope Linus II out of the plane.

Bishop Harbinger hurried over to greet the pope as His Holiness brushed dust off his white cassock.

"Bishop Harbinger, it is good to see you," said the pope. "I understand Mr. Slocum is about to fly off to Woomba to bring in the two foreign ministers."

"Yes, Your Holiness. We'll make sure the herons will not cause any problems with Slocum's second landing. By the way, I thought Fides was coming with you?"

"He did. Where in heaven's name is he?"

Slocum jumped up on the wing of his Piper Cub.

"He's hiding down here. I think the landing frightened him."

Slocum lifted Fides out of the cockpit. When the pilot put Fides down on the ground, the dog jumped back into the plane. A candy bar finally enticed Fides back out of the cockpit.

* * * * * *

Although it was close to midday, Pope Linus began to walk to Lipoppo.

Harbinger stopped him. "Holiness, it is a long walk to the village. It is very hot. Let Obani drive you in our Range Rover."

"No, I ride in cars every day. I wish to walk outside and meet the people."

"Then at least ride a bicycle."

"I do not have a bike. I'll have to borrow one from a villager."

"Your Holiness. I would be honored if you would take mine. My mother and father gave it to me when I was a child. Whenever I ride it, I think of them."

"Then it is I who am honored."

Delighted crowds cheered as the Holy Father and Bishop Harbinger pedaled along the road toward Lipoppo with Fides sitting in a basket on the back of the pope's bicycle. As they reached the outskirts of the village, the pope stopped.

"Bishop Samuel, I remember the story you told me about the boy Gabriel and his elephants."

"Yes, the boy died of AIDS in our clinic."

"Take me to the clinic so I can say a prayer for him."

"The nurse will be angry if I brought you there without giving her advance notice. She would want to dress the children in their best clothes, and if there were time, teach them a welcoming speech."

"I bring God's blessing. It needs no advance notice to be effective."

* * * * * *

That night, the Council of Elders hosted a dinner for the pope and the two ministers. Slocum was invited as well. During the dinner, Harbinger studied the ministers carefully. They were a study in contrasts. The Israeli Minister, Jacob Dayer, was a man who looked like he had been put together with spare parts—he had a big head, narrow shoulders, long arms, a protruding belly, and thick stubby legs. Palestinian Minister, Mahmood Mylas, on the other hand, was elegant in the extreme. He was tall and broad shouldered with long expressive fingers—the fingers of a pianist someone once said—a round, boyish face and a broad smile. There was, however, a scrubbed, almost antiseptic, look about Mylas that many found off-putting and some even sinister. Despite their differences in looks and demeanor, however, the two men shared one characteristic. Both men were tough, no-nonsense negotiators.

After coffee, Pope Linus excused himself. It had been a long flight from Rome to Lipoppo. Harbinger escorted the pope to his quarters. Slocum tried to interest the ministers in some brandy. Mylas and Dayer both demurred. When they left, Slocum continued drinking late into the night. Finally the pilot staggered into the cockpit of his Piper Cub and passed out.

* * * * * *

At five o'clock the next morning, Obani drove the Range Rover to the back door of the rectory. While Bagua served coffee and muffins to Pope Linus and the others, Obani filled the trunk of the van with food, bottled water, medical supplies and two spare tires. When the Range Rover was fully packed, Obani tapped on the horn to signal that he was ready to drive out to the water hole. The pope took the front seat with Fides asleep in his lap. The two ministers and Biahop Harbinger sat in the back. The ride out to the water hole was uneventful. While Obani parked the Range Rover, Bishop Harbinger took the pope and the ministers for a walk down to the edge of the water hole. Fides remained in the Range Rover.

Jacob Dayer pickrd up a stone and tried to throw it to the other side of the water. It fell short by sieveral meters.

Mylas picked up another stone and threw it easily to the other side.of the water hole.

Bishop Harbinger defused an awkward moment with some levity. "In my gut, I knew we'd have a rocky start to our discussions."

By now it was almost daybreak and the animals were stirring. A small herd of wildebeest walked down to the water's edge. Just behind them came a herd of gazelles.

Harbinger spoke in a muffled voice. "I think it's time to start back to our observation deck. Be careful not to trip over something in the path."As they walked back, two lions, a male and female, stepped out of the tall grass and stood in the path.

Bishop Harbinger smiled. "It's a welcoming committee. I told Banda, the male, about Pope Linus - that he was the head of the Catholic Church with one billion members."

Banda walked towards the pope, "Don't be afraid, Holiness, He's curious. He won't harm you. Just rub him on the head. He likes that."

Jacob Dayer handed Bishop Harbinger a camera. "Do you think you could take a picture of me and this Banda friend of yours? My kids would love to have it."

"Of course. I'll take a picture for you too, Mahmood."

After a few minutes, the lions seemed to lose interest and disappeared into the grass.

The pope asked Bishop Harbinger "Will we see Banda again?"

"I think so."

* * * * * *

When they had walked back to the viewing platform, Mahmood Mylas began to climb onto the platform ahead of Pope Linus. Jacob Dayer went to stop him. "Pope Linus should go first, Mylas. He's our host, or doesn't that matter to you?"

The pope signaled Mylas to continue up the steps. "We'll alternate who goes up first and who comes down first. It'll be our own water hole rule."

As the day progressed, many different species of animals came down to the water hole to drink. Zebras, gazelles, wildebeests, water buffalos, cheetahs, jackals—the list grew longer by the hour. Lounging drowsily under a stand of nearby trees was Banda and his pride of lions. Harbinger pointed them out. "They usually drink at night and spend a good part of the day resting. Only the elephant dares challenge the lion to supremacy over the water hole."

After lunch, several impalas came down to drink. Just beyond the impalas, a hippo broke the surface of the water.

Mahmood Mylas, the Palestinian foreign minister, borrowed a pair of binoculars from Obani. He watched the gray green figure glide slowly around the pool, its eyes watching the movement of the other animals. Mylas lay the binoculars on the table and opened a bottle of water. "I wouldn't want to run into the likes of him if I were taking a swim. He has meanness written all over him."

An hour later, Bishop Harbinger noticed movement in the grass.

"We are in luck. We are about to receive a visit from the most dangerous predator of them all—the leopard. Some might call him the misanthrope of the animal kingdom."

"Why a misanthrope, Samuel?" asked Pope Linus.

"The leopard lives alone, hunts alone, and feeds alone. Unlike its rivals, the lion, or the cheetah, the leopard usually hoists his prey into a tree and eats it there. He wants no uninvited guests."

The leopard came out of the grass and walked down to the water hole. A small herd of zebra moved away from the leopard as it walked into the water hole and started to drink.

"My friends, you are witnessing the fundamental rule of the water hole. It is a place that is off-limits to killing."

"Amazing!" Jacob Dayer, the Israeli foreign minister's eyes opened wide. "You can be told a hundred times that animals do not kill at a water hole but to see a leopard and zebras drinking a few meters from one another really brings the message home."

"It's ultimately a question of survival." Bishop Harbinger adjusted his umbrella to block out more of the sun. "If the leopard killed at the water hole, the leftover carcass would start to putrefy and become a feast for scavengers. It wouldn't take long before carrion would pile up and the water would become poisoned. Once that happened, the animals would have to leave."

As the leopard finished drinking and turned to leave, a herd of elephants strode out of the tall grass. They headed straight for the water hole and began to splash, and spray one another with their trunks. Suddenly, trumpeting its pain, a lone bull elephant with a pair of broken tusks burst out of the grass and headed pell-mell toward the water hole. When he reached the edge of the water, the rogue swayed back and forth as if he were listening to sounds emanating from the bowels of the earth. Then flapping his ears and lifting his trunk, the rogue bellowed loudly and plunged headlong into the water. He started butting a female elephant to try to separate her from the herd. A group of bulls would have none of that, however. They formed a circle around the female and drove the rogue away whenever he tried to reach her.

Sensing that he was not going to have his way, the rogue ran toward a herd of gazelles feeding on the edge of the water hole. The gazelles turned and ran from the elephant as it came closer. The unexpected departure of the gazelles started something akin to a chain reaction. A herd of zebras ran off followed by groups of wildebeests and antelope. Even Banda and his pride shook off their afternoon drowsiness and left the shade of the trees. Soon the water hole was empty, leaving the bull elephant alone with its anger.

Bishop Harbinger spoke first. "Gentlemen, you have just seen a rogue elephant—they are savages and will kill to get whatever it is they want. Notice how the rest of the herd shuns the rogue and tries to drive him away. They will not let him stay part of the group."

The pope stood up and drank some water. "Look at what effect that one rogue elephant has had on the life of the water hole. All

121

of the animals have left for fear of that one elephant. Africa is a guileless land. It hides nothing from you."

Jacob Dayer walked to the edge of the viewing deck.

"With all due respect for my colleague from Palestine, substitute the word Hamas, or Hezbollah for the words rogue elephant and you have in microcosm the problem of Jerusalem. The rogues are in control and nobody dares do anything about it. They should be ostracized, not embraced. Until that occurs, the Jewish people will have to defend themselves."

The Palestinian minister bridled. "This Jew has the audacity to sit here and talk about defending himself. In his vocabulary, defending himself means taking land at gunpoint from Palestinians and then forcing them to live like animals in Gaza and in parts of the West Bank. And oh, I forgot. If Israel goes too far in defending itself, it simply calls its lobbyists in Washington to gather the necessary support for what it is doing."

"Gentlemen, we are not going to make much progress by using rhetoric like that." Pope Linus sensed it was time to cool tempers. "Let me also emphasize that Washington is not a party to these negotiations. I spoke to Gilbert Cleverhand, the U.S. secretary of state, and he agrees."

Mylas laughed derisively. "How can Washington claim it's not a party to these negotiations? Israel has the support of the United States in everything it does. We are a nation-in-waiting, and we will continue in that capacity until Washington changes its policy. As for not making much progress, let me be a contrarian. We have made enormous progress. We've been talking for several hours and Dayer hasn't dusted off old Holocaust pictures to get our sympathies."

Dayer shot back. "Millions of Jews were slaughtered in the Holocaust. A Jew does not 'dust' off pictures of the genocide. It is an open wound."

Mylas smirked. "Some scholars say the Holocaust never took place."

Jacob Dayer stood and started to put his papers into his satchel.

"Thank you for your hospitality, Your Holiness. But I see no reason for me to stay here and listen to this. Certain things were not meant to be, and I'm afraid peace in Jerusalem is one of them. Bishop Harbinger, could you arrange for me to fly back to Nairobi tonight?"

"Not tonight, Mr. Minister. There is no electricity in either the Lipoppo or the Woomba Airports. It would be too dangerous to take off without light."

"What about a car and driver?"

"The road to Nairobi is full of sinkholes. It is risky to drive it at night. Wait until the morning."

"I seem to have no choice in the matter." The Israeli minister dialed his cell phone. "Even if I leave early in the morning, I should be able to go to my daughter's piano recital later in the day."

"Gentlemen, before all of this totally unravels, I hope you will not disappoint Obani. He has been planning for days to give you a tour of the savannah north of here."

Dayer nodded. "Well then, we have the time. There's no need to disappoint your driver. I'll be happy to take the tour."

"I won't spoil the party." Like Dayer, Mylas started packing his belongings. "But I would also like to leave for Nairobi as soon as possible tomorrow morning."

Pleased that the two ministers had agreed to the tour, Harbinger called to Obani.

"Bring over the cans of the new bug repellant. The ads say it is twice as powerful as what is already on the market. We should spray ourselves liberally with the repellant. At this time of day, the mosquitoes are vicious on the grasslands. We want no one catching malaria."

As proxy for the others, Pope Linus asked Harbinger a question. "If we leave the platform, will the repellant attract the rogue? The spray has a particularly pungent odor."

Harbinger smiled reassuringly. "Unless we do something to provoke him, an elephant, even one as big as the rogue, will not attack a vehicle the size of a Range Rover."

The pope and bishop got into the Range Rover first. The two ministers sat next to each other, talking on their cell phones. Obani turned on the ignition. He drove the vehicle north onto the open savannah.

"Are there rhinos in this area, Obani?" the pope asked the postman.

"Yes, Holy Father, but there are not many. It is because of the big game hunters. A rhino horn brings a big price in Asia. The hunters also come to kill elephants and lions."

After about an hour's ride, Obani drove back to the water hole. Mahmood Mylas got out of the Range Rover first but stood at the bottom of the steps up to the platform.

"Pope Linus, it's your turn to go up first."

"Thank you, Mr. Minister. I'll take Fides up with me."

Once the pope had climbed up, Mylas went second. As the Israeli minister walked over to the steps, he tripped and twisted his ankle.

"Are you okay?" Pope Linus called down to Dayer.

"I think so.. I don't think the ankle's broken. I'll be okay in a couple of minutes."

As Dayer started to limp to the ladder, there was a sound of something crashing through the bushes. The rogue elephant burst out into the open and headed directly toward the Range Rover.

Obani slammed the doors shut. "He's going to ram us. Pope Linus was right. The smell of the repellant must have attracted the elephant."

Lowering its head, the elephant crashed into the side of the Range Rover and tried to turn it on its side. The vehicle balanced precariously as the bull rammed it a second time. The rogue was preparing to ram the Range Rover again when it saw Dayer trying desperately to climb up the ladder to the safety of the platform. Trumpeting loudly, the rogue ran toward the Israeli minister.

"Jacob, stop moving. An elephant has poor eyesight."

Mahmood Mylas jumped down from the platform to help Dayer climb up the ladder. The rogue continued to run toward Dayer and now, Mylas.

Suddenly, Banda and two lionesses came hurtling out of the grass. Dayer couldn't believe his eyes. Banda's charge, as the Israeli minister would later describe it, reminded him of one of those scenes in a Hollywood movie where at the last minute, the cavalry comes to the rescue of a wagon train.

The three lions circled around the rogue confusing him and making him dizzy. Although Fides did not leave the platform, he produced a volume of high-pitched yelping noises that seemed to particularly irritate the elephant. While Banda and the other lions kept the rogue preoccupied, Mylas managed to help Dayer climb up the steps of the ladder. Harbinger and Obani also got out of the Range Rover and escaped up the ladder. Their purpose achieved, the lions ran back into the grass.

Dayer looked at his Palestinian colleague.

"Mahmood, why did you risk your life for a Jew?"

"I helped you because you are a father, not because you are a Jew. I have a daughter, too."

Fingering his gold pectoral cross, Pope Linus looked determined to make his point.

"Gentlemen, we have just been treated to our own private lesson in terrorism. What united us was stronger than what divided us. This is the message that must be brought to both your governments. We all need the courage and resolve to suppress terrorism in all its forms. Unless you do it, there will never be peace in Jerusalem. I say this recognizing that my own church has hardly been a model for rooting out extremists—the Inquisition and the Crusades were done with the full support of the papacy."

"Since the Holy Father has spoken so forthrightly, so will I." Mylas, the Palestinian minister, stood and paced along the edge of the platform. "It will not be easy to root out terrorists in Gaza and the West Bank. Resentment against Jews runs deep. Many groups in the population support terrorists because they benefit from the death of Jews. Some would cheer a second Holocaust if they could profit from it."

The Israeli minister poured a glass of water. "Many Jews like to think we're somehow immune from prejudice, that we are morally superior to the rest of the world. If a Jew were to look deep inside him, however, he may discover things that he would prefer not knowing."

"Like what?" Harbinger pressed the Israeli foreign minister to be specific.

"Some Israelis believe that Arabs have no rights—they should be treated like wild animals."

After the Israeli minister made his point, there was an awkward silence. Samuel Harbinger suddenly cocked his ear and smiled. "Do you hear that drumming sound off in the distance?"

The three men nodded.

"It is the sound of hoof beats. The zebras are coming back to take their accustomed places at the water hole."

Pope Linus looked quizzically at Harbinger. "How can you be sure it's zebras, Samuel? The hoof beats are so far away."

"Holiness, the sound of a herd of zebras is unmistakable. They run as if they have never learned to walk."

Minutes later, the first of the herd of zebras thundered out of the high grass and splashed into the water.

As the men stood watching the zebras, the Israeli foreign minister pointed toward the stand of trees.

"Look who is returning to reclaim their position as rulers of the water hole."

A lioness carrying a cub by the nape of the neck walked out of the grass and took her accustomed place under the stand of trees. Behind her strode Banda, nudging a second cub to follow its mother. Several minutes later, a second lioness arrived with two cubs.

The Israeli foreign minister borrowed a pair of binoculars. "The royal family is back in residence."

The Palestinian minister took a deep breath. "Sometimes, I envision those of us who live in the Middle East as swimmers swept along by an undertow that we can't control. The more we push ahead, the more we are pulled back. Pope Linus is right. We have to take steps to control terrorism in our countries or it will control us. I may live to regret this, but I will recommend to my government that we continue these discussions. All of us have experienced how a rogue can make one fear for his life."

The Israeli minister nodded in assent. "I will make the same recommendation."

* * * * * *

The four men left the viewing platform late in the day. The pope was scheduled to say Mass in the village at 7:00 PM. As they rode back to Lipoppo, the main road into the village was clogged with people. As Obani inched the Range Rover through the crowd, Pope Linus and Bishop Harbinger climbed up on the roof of the truck and waved to the thousands of people. When they saw the pope, the women clapped their hands and began to dance, their brightly colored skirts swirling about in a blaze of color. As more and more people joined in the dance, the women made high clicking sounds as they whirled about in circles at a faster and faster rate. To the pope, the music was infectious, and it wasn't long before he found himself swaying to the rhythms of East Africa.

"Samuel, we danced once in St. Peter's, but I have never seen dancing like this before."

"In Africa, we dance to express what's in our hearts. We dance when we are happy and we dance when we are sad. Today, we dance in joy because God's Vicar has come among us."

When the pope reached Lipoppo, the crowds had grown even larger. They threw flowers and pushed forward to touch the pope as he climbed down from the roof of the Range Rover. Bishop

Harbinger hurried the pontiff into the rectory to avoid being crushed by the throng.

Father Cropsy had laid out the papal vestments for the upcoming liturgy. Pope Linus put his hand on Bishop Harbinger's shoulder.

"Do me one favor, Samuel. Hurry up and grow older. With some gray hairs, it will be easier to introduce your brand of Christianity to Catholics in other parts of the world. Tell me, Samuel. What do you wear when you say Mass?"

"I must confess, Holy Father, I usually say Mass in a dashiki or in a white shirt and dark pants. Somehow wearing vestments embroidered with gold makes me feel cut off from my parishioners."

"Samuel, I will wear a dashiki to say Mass. You are right—vestments embroidered with gold thread are made for Masses in St. Peter's not for Masses here in Lipoppo.

As the sun began to set, the drums grew louder.

"Samuel, before Mass begins, I want you to hear my confession."

Samuel Harbinger waas stunned.

"Holy Father, I cannot hear your confession. I am not worthy. You are the pope."

"But a pope who ridiculed what you said and did – a pope who would have stripped you of your episcoplal powers had that been possible. I have sinned, Samuel. Hear my confession.".

Harbinger choked with emotion.

"I will, Holy Father if that is your wish. Come with me into the church."

The drums of Africa grew louder as the time for Mass approached..

* * * * * *

When Pope Linus walked out on the altar, he stopped and

stood thoughtfully for a moment. The people stood quietly and waited for him to speak.

"I will pray at Mass tonight for two intentions. First, that what we have started here today represents a new beginning for peace in Jerusalem, and second, that God may smile on the people of Africa and lift the yoke of poverty and disease off their backs. I will add a special prayer of my own for the people of Lipoppo and for their bishop, Samuel Harbinger, from whom I have learned so much."

Bishop Harbinger, Ignatius Cropsy, and Father Albert stood next to the pope and concelebrated the Mass. The two foreign ministers took the seats of honor on either side of the outdoor altar.

For the Gospel reading, the pope chose a passage from Saint Matthew—a story about a blind man whose eyesight is restored by Jesus. After the pope read the Gospel, children from Lipoppo and Woomba, led by Zamba's teenage son, carried the gifts of bread and wine up to the pope. The Holy Father took the offerings and blessed each of the children. Seeing his son standing next to the pope brought tears to Zamba's eyes.

After the children left the altar, Bagua and Lacata, the woman from Woomba, poured water over the pope's hands as he prepared to perform the Sacred Eucharist. Father Albert had asked Bishop Samuel if Lacata could help perform the ablutions with Bagua. "She recently lost her son," Samuel agreed.

When it was time for the Eucharist, everyone wanted to receive the consecrated bread from Pope Linus.

Bishop Harbinger whispered in the pope's ear. "Holy Father, you cannot distribute the Eucharist to so large a crowd."

"Many have traveled great distances to come to Mass and to greet me, Samuel. I will not disappoint them."

Bishop Harbinger and his fellow priests tried to keep order in the communion line. Despite the ban on animals, children carried their pets to meet Pope Linus. Bowing to the inevitable, the pope blessed dogs, and cats and gazelles and snakes—even a baby hyena. Bagua's six-year-old daughter cried when the pope would not give communion to her water buffalo.

When Mass was over, the crowds that had come to greet the pope cheered as he blessed them. Tired by the events of the day, Pope Linus went to the rectory to sleep. Drums sounded late into the night in honor of Lipoppo's honored guest.

* * * * * *

The next morning, Duke Rayner was treated to an impromptu interview with an ebullient Pope Linus as the pontiff waited for Slocum's plane to fly him to Nairobi.

"Your Holiness, as you leave Lipoppo this morning, how would you characterize the state of the negotiations?"

"Given the intervention of a new party, I am optimistic?"

"New party? What new party?"

"The Holy Spirit.. He can be terribly persuasive when he wants to be."

"So you think the Holy Spirit will bring peace to Jerusalem?"

"Let's see what he does."

Just then Slocum turned on the motor of his piper club. When Fides heard the plane, he started to whimper.

Pope Linus smiled. "It won't be too bad, Fides."

Fides disagreed. He howled and whimpered all the way to Nairobi.

* * * * * *

After the Holy Father had left Lipoppo, Bishop Harbinger accompanied the two ministers to Woomba where planes waited to take them home...

As Jacob Dayer was about to board his plane, he embraced the bishop.

"Rememer those two stones near the water hole, you were right about them. The road was rocky at first, but now we are only a stone's throw away from a major breakthrough in combating terrorism."

As Harbinge and Obani drove back to Lipoppo, the bishop saw Banda sitting forlornly along the road.

"Stop the car, Obani."

Harbinger walked over to where Banda was sitting.

"I'm sorry. With all the excitement, I forgot to tell you all that happrnrd."

Banda started to walk away.

"If I give you a chocolate bar, will you let me explain?"

Banda kept walking."

"If I give you two chocolate bars, then will you let me explain?"

Banda kept walking but at a slightly slower pace."

"Okay, three.chocolate bars."

Banda stopped and growled.

"You drive one hard bargain, Banda. Okay, one chocolate bar for each of your lionesses in addition to your three."

* * * * * *

A week later, an early morning phone call came into Lipoppo. Luckily, Obani had already started sorting the mail and took the call.

"This is Christina Hagerbloom calling from Oslo, Norway. Is Bishop Harbinger there?"

"No, I'm sorry, ma'am. The bishop is still sleeping. Could you call him back later today?"

"No, it's urgent. We are trying to arrange a conference call with Pope Linus in Rome and with Bishop Samuel in Lipoppo. It's important."

"Then you'll have to wait until I bike over to the rectory to get him up."

"Go ahead. Tell him the woman who borrowed his cassock in Rome is calling."

Minutes later, Bishop Harbinger picked up the phone.

"Christina, how are you? I'm still half asleep."

"I apologize for the early morning call, but we're trying to get you and Pope Linus on the line together."

"Why?"

Suddenly, the phone clicked and Pope Linus joined the conversation.

"Your Holiness and Bishop Harbinger—you both might wish to take a seat."

"Why, Christina?" Harbinger looked puzzled.

"Both of you have been awarded the Nobel Peace Prize. Congratulations."

"But Christina, why are *you* calling Pope Linus and me to announce the award?"

"In all the excitement in Rome, I guess I forgot to tell you that I work for the Nobel Peace Prize Committee. And I guess I also forgot to tell you the prize comes with a one point six million dollar stipend. I assume each of you will receive one half?"

"No," Pope Linus spoke. "My share will go to Bishop Harbinger to help build a new AIDS clinic in Lipoppo. The gift is given in honor of the boy named Gabriel."

Chapter Eight
A Reception in Oslo

A military honor guard snapped to attention as King Haakon V of Norway bounded down the steps of Oslo City Hall to greet his honored guest—His Excellency, Samuel Harbinger, bishop of Lipoppo, Kenya. The Nobel Peace Prize had been awarded jointly to Pope Linus II and to Bishop Harbinger for their work in building peace in the Holy City of Jerusalem. Pope Linus had declined to come to Oslo to accept the award in person. Bishop Harbinger, however, agreed to accept the award on behalf of both laureates.

Lanky, with sandy-colored hair and blue eyes, the king was what people would expect a sixty-year-old King of Norway to look like. So, too, with her alabaster complexion and green eyes, Charlotte, the queen consort, was what a fifty-seven-year-old Norwegian queen consort would look like.

Smiling broadly, the king walked to the podium.

"On behalf of the people of Norway, Bishop Harbinger, I bid you welcome. Your trip here to accept the Nobel Peace Prize has become not only a media event, but also an event that has swelled the pride of the Norwegian people. Here in Oslo City Hall—not fifty meters from where we sit—is a retrospective on Thor Heyerdahl and his journeys on the *Kon Tiki* and the *Ra*. Ibsen festivals have sprouted up in many towns and villages throughout the country. Attendance at the Edvard Munch Museum here in Oslo has broken all records. Last night in Bergen, tickets for an Edvard Grieg concert were sold out in a matter of hours. The same thing happened the week before in Stavanger.

"I see the queen is signaling me to introduce our laureate not to brag about the people of Norway. As always, Queen Charlotte is right.

"This year the Nobel Peace Prize has been shared by two men, Pope Linus II and Bishop Samuel Harbinger. So with all available trumpets, I present to you our Nobel Peace Prize Laureate, Samuel Harbinger, who with Pope Linus took what everyone thought was impossible and showed us that it was possible."

Bishop Harbinger walked up to the podium. A library step had been provided so the bishop could see over the bank of microphones.

"It is with a sense of awe that I stand before this glittering assembly tonight. In front of me, sit kings and queens, presidents and prime ministers, scientists and scholars from all over the world. I am particularly honored that the secretary general of the United Nations has joined us tonight.

"As I look out over this audience, I ask myself what I could possibly say that would interest such a distinguished assembly. I am a simple priest from a small village in Kenya. I know little science and even less literature. I admit to studying Latin in the seminary but with what success you'll have to be the judge. I'm still not sure whether the *Aeneid* was written by Caesar or by Ovid."

The bishop's self-deprecating humor relaxed the audience.

"As I flew here to Oslo yesterday from Nairobi, I thought back over these last eventful months. Foreign ministers Dayer and

Mylas have managed to convince their respective governments to take meaningful steps toward peace. The rules of the water hole have been effective models for building a lasting peace. Much has been accomplished, but much more needs to be done.

"To build a lasting peace in Jerusalem, I was reminded of a story about two stonemasons—let us call them Axam and Axum.

"One day a wise king, much like our host King Haakon, called his stonemasons to his palace. The king commanded each of them to build him a stone corral. 'Whoever finishes his corral first,' the king said, 'I will give him a bonus of fifty gold coins.'

"Axam took round stones and piled them one on top of the other. He finished building his corral in three days. Axum, however, took broken stones and carefully fit them into one another. Axum took ten days to build his corral.

"When both had finished, the king called Axam and Axum back to his palace.

"'I said I would pay a bonus of fifty gold coins to the one who finished his corral first. Axam, you built your corral in three days, and Axum, you built yours in ten. We must wait until the first rain before I pay out the fifty gold coins.'

"'Why?' said Axam. 'I built mine first.'

"'But we must see if what you built was actually a corral," the king answered.

"A week later, a rainstorm fell on the city. The next morning, the king walked out to the corrals. The force of the rain had toppled the round stones of Axam's corral. The force of the rain, however, had not toppled the broken stones on Axum's corral. The king gave the fifty gold coins to Axum."

Bishop Harbinger sipped a glass of water.

"To build a lasting peace in Jerusalem, we can learn much from the story of the two stonemasons. To build his corral, Axam took the easy path—he piled round stones one on top of another. Axum took the harder path—he fitted broken stones one into the other. When the rains came, Axam's round stones rolled off each other, but Axum's stones held firm. To bring peace to Jerusalem, easy solutions like Axam's round stones will not work. Complex, well-planned solutions like Axum's stones, however, will. Fit into one another, they created a solid structure kept together by their own weight. So to build peace, we must make hundreds, and yes, even thousands of linkages between Jews and Palestinians. This process will be slow and complex but in the end, it will be successful. God bless the people of Jerusalem and the people of Norway."

At the reception after the award ceremony, Bishop Harbinger met many people including the president of Harvard University and the secretary general of the United Nations. As is the custom at such events, he handed out many business cards and accepted many more in return.

Chapter Nine
A Trip to New York

There was a feeling of expectancy in the air as the sleek Boeing 747 emblazoned with the Stars and Stripes touched down on a remote runway at New York's John F. Kennedy International Airport.

Cyprus-born Basil Theocritus, the secretary general of the United Nations, had invited Samuel Harbinger, Nobel laureate and Bishop of Lipoppo, to address the General Assembly. At Theocritus' request, the president of the United States had dispatched a plane to Nairobi to bring the bishop to New York City. Security was unusually tight at the airport. Threats had been received on Bishop Harbinger's life. Every guest was thoroughly searched and all bags opened. Police dogs sniffed suspicious items.

* * * * * *

Kevin Larkin, deputy inspector of the New York City Police Department, was rapidly losing his patience. The 747 was taxiing to a halt on the JFK runway, but the mayor's office and the New

York archdiocese were still at loggerheads over arrangements for the receiving line. While both parties agreed that, the secretary general should be the first to greet the bishop, the two protocol officers, Monsignor Philip "Spooky" Crenshaw from the archdiocese, and Seth Benjamin from the mayor's office, could not agree on who should be second.

Larkin could barely control his Irish temper. "The plane has landed. You guys got exactly two minutes to resolve this or I will."

"Kevin, don't threaten me," Spooky Crenshaw shot back at Larkin. "Save your bullying for Seth. He's the one being unreasonable."

Friend and foe alike called Phil Crenshaw, Spooky. No one, not even Crenshaw himself, could remember the origins of the nickname. Crenshaw did admit once to a friend that it probably had something to do with a devil costume he wore as a child trick or treating on Halloween. "The costume would terrify many children, sending them running home to their mothers," he had said.

"Spooky, cut the crap, will you? Harbinger's invitation to address the General Assembly did not come from the archdiocese. It came from the United Nations. Theocritus comes first, then the mayor, and then the archbishop."

"But you seem to forget one thing, Seth. The guest is a bishop, as in Roman Catholic bishop."

"Don't patronize me with that tone of voice, Spooky."

"I'm not patronizing you, Seth. Facts are facts. The United States has diplomatic relations with the Holy See. Cardinal Plimpton is not only Archbishop of New York; he's also one of the pope's advisors and a prince of the Catholic Church. What comparable diplomatic rank does the mayor have?"

"You can recite Plimpton's titles and privileges until you're blue in the face. But I can tell you one thing—when this Bishop Harbinger gets off the plane, the mayor, not the cardinal, is going to be standing next to the secretary general on that goddamned receiving line."

Larkin interrupted. "Try this on for size. I assume His Eminence knows the bishop."

Monsignor Crenshaw nodded. "Yes, he's met the bishop in Rome. Plimpton has even donated money to Harbinger for a new AIDS clinic."

"Have Cardinal Plimpton invited onto the plane in an unofficial capacity. He wants to greet a friend and fellow bishop. Plimpton can walk with the bishop down the stairs. The mayor will be number two on the receiving line and everybody should be happy," said Larkin.

"That would work for us." Monsignor Crenshaw looked relieved at the suggestion.

"And it works for us." Benjamin cleared his throat. "As long as the mayor is number two on the receiving line, I don't care what goes on inside the plane or who follows the bishop down the stairs."

When the 747 had come to a halt, a ground crew pushed a mobile staircase up to the door of the aircraft. The cardinal clambered up the steps and disappeared through the door of the plane.

A few minutes later, Bishop Harbinger, dressed in a black and white dashiki, emerged from the plane, and began to descend the stairs. Behind him came Cardinal Plimpton balancing a platter full of cookies in one hand and holding the rail with the other. At the bottom of the staircase stood Basil Theocritus, the secretary general of the United Nations.

Suddenly, four jet aircraft in tight formation thundered across the sky. As the planes passed over the 747 parked on the JFK runway, they flipped on their backs and roared off to the east.

Bishop Harbinger looked frightened. "Are the planes going to attack us?"

Plimpton laughed. "They are the Blue Angels, the United States Navy's precision flying team. They are here to give you a big 'hello' from the people of the United States. They're going to do one more flyover. This time it'll involve six planes. The maneuver is called the Delta Formation. Here they come."

The planes flew in from the north at almost treetop level. As they passed over the 747, the planes veered off in different directions. Then with full throttles, the Blue Angels climbed straight up into the sky.

In the excitement of watching the Delta Formation, the cardinal went to give a "thumbs-up" to the pilots, forgetting the tray of cookies balanced in his hand. The platter crashed on the ramp, sending broken cookies raining down on a startled mayor and his wife.

Chagrined, Plimpton pulled out his handkerchief and ran down the remaining steps of the staircase. He began brushing vanilla frosting off the mayor's blue pinstripe suit. "Mr. Mayor, I apologize. I forgot I was carrying the tray. The cookies were gifts from Bishop Harbinger's housekeeper named Bagua."

When all the frosting and colored sprinkles had been cleaned off the mayor and his wife, the secretary general walked up to a podium that stood on the tarmac to the right of the staircase. He motioned the audience to take their seats for the welcoming ceremony.

"I'm sure that our honored guest, Bishop Harbinger, did not foresee the rather unconventional welcoming ceremony we have provided him. The mayor of our city is usually prepared to be 'battered' by the press but not by the archbishop."

Secretary Theocritus' quip produced roars of laughter and a red-faced Cardinal Plimpton. The secretary general raised his hands to quiet the guests.

"I was extraordinarily privileged to meet Bishop Harbinger several months ago in Oslo at the Nobel Peace Prize reception. In my capacity as Secretary General of the United Nations, I have met almost every world leader and captain of industry alive today. Few have made a deeper impression on me than this simple priest from the village of Lipoppo in Kenya. I could say much more about this man, but I'll let him speak for himself. In my native Cyprus, we say that an introduction should last no longer than it takes to drink a glass of water—and a small one at that. So having taken enough time, I welcome my friend to the United Nations."

The secretary general turned to yield the podium to Bishop Harbinger, but the bishop was nowhere to be seen.

"What happened to Samuel?" Secretary Theocritus asked Deputy Inspector Larkin.

"I don't know. He was here a minute ago."

"There he is." Monsignor Crenshaw pointed to several police officers standing on the tarmac. Bishop Harbinger's dashiki was clearly visible among them.

Theocritus fumed. "Someone get Samuel over here. He's violating protocol."

Crenshaw ran over to where Harbinger was standing with the police. "Your Excellency, we need you over there at the bottom of the ramp to respond to Theocritus' welcome and then greet the invited guests."

"I'll be there in a minute. The planes frightened the police dogs. I'm trying to help their handlers calm them down."

"But the secretary general's guests are waiting. You are embarrassing him."

"Okay, I'm coming."

The bishop ran over to the end of the receiving line and started shaking hands. Spooky Crenshaw tapped Harbinger on the shoulder.

"Bishop Harbinger, the receiving line starts at the bottom of the stairs, not here."

Harbinger looked baffled. "As long as I shake everyone's hand, does it really matter in what order I do it?"

Spooky Crenshaw nodded. "Unfortunately, at the United Nations, it does. There are rules of protocol for diplomats just like there are rules of liturgy for priests. Both sets of rules must be rigidly adhered to."

"Well then, Monsignor, get me to the right place to begin. I did not realize that by helping an animal, I was precipitating an international incident."

* * * * * *

There was a rumor that Bishop Harbinger had asked to visit the New York Stock Exchange and Ground Zero on his way from JFK Airport to Cardinal Plimpton's residence in Midtown Manhattan. The New York City Police Department, of course, refused to confirm that the bishop was in the city, let alone publish his route from JFK into Manhattan. Despite the official news blackout, however, the New York *Daily News* printed a detailed description of the bishop's itinerary from the airport to the cardinal's residence.

One might ask how the *Daily News* came by its information. The short answer is that New Yorkers have an inability to keep secrets—at least in the conventional sense of these words. To most inhabitants of the Big Apple, keeping a secret meant telling only one person at a time. Another group of New Yorkers, however, objected to secrecy on philosophical grounds. The very concept of keeping a secret, they thought, violated the First Amendment to the United States Constitution. In such an environment, it is not surprising that even the most closely guarded information quickly finds its way to a reporter.

In the case of Bishop Harbinger's route into Manhattan, Seth Benjamin from the mayor's office let the information slip to his acupuncturist, who just happened to repeat it to his girlfriend, who in turn told it to a member of her book club, who told it to her regular squash partner, who told it to his next door neighbor, who repeated it to a reporter for the *Daily News*. At least this seems to be the most widely accepted version of the facts.

* * * * * *

The New York City police had three options to bring Bishop

Harbinger from JFK to the stock exchange—limousine, helicopter, or ferry. At the last minute, the police decided to "chopper" the bishop into Lower Manhattan. At a heliport on the East River, the bishop transferred to a bulletproof limousine for a quick ride to the New York Stock Exchange.

Harbinger's unannounced appearance on the balcony of the exchange set off wild applause. The president of the exchange asked him to say a few words. Harbinger thought a moment and agreed.

"From the companies represented here, I hope that a cure for AIDS will come soon. Africa is dying and our hope is with you."

To the consternation of his security guards, the bishop asked to walk out on the floor of the exchange. He startled most of the traders when he knelt down and kissed the ground. As he left, someone started to cheer, "Lipoppo for Pope."

From the stock exchange, there was a quick limousine ride to Ground Zero, the place where the Twin Towers' collapsed. His brother Vincent met him at the site. The mayor described the horror of that day. When the mayor had finished, children from schools in the Roman Catholic Archdiocese read a list of the names of the dead.

Bishop Harbinger stood listening to the recitation of names. He whispered to his brother, "It reminds me of the Litany of the Saints."

"It is a litany of saints all right, but it's a litany of twenty-first century saints killed by terrorists."

In a cavalcade of police cars and limousines, Bishop Harbinger left Ground Zero, and he was driven to Cardinal Plimpton's residence in Midtown.

* * * * * *

The next morning, Bishop Samuel Harbinger rose at 4:00 AM. He slipped quietly out of Cardinal Plimpton's residence and walked to Fifth Avenue. As he passed St. Patrick's Cathedral, he saw an elderly man hobble up the steps of the church. The man tried to push open the church doors, but they had not yet been unlocked. Pulling his coat around him, the man sat on the ground and waited for the church to open. Harbinger thought it strange that churches in America were not open all day and night.

A church is not a nine to five business, he thought.

At the corner of Fifty-seventh Street and Fifth Avenue, he stopped to watch sanitation workers empty a large metal dumpster.

One of the sanitation workers walked over to where Harbinger was standing. "Good morning, Father. Have you ever seen a dumpster being unloaded?"

"No."

"Well, you're about to see it now." A garbage truck hoisted the metal bin into the air and shook its contents into the truck.

"So much for Tiffany's refuse. By the way, Father, why are you up and about so early?"

"I'm heading for the Bronx Zoo. Do you know how to get there?"

"It's pretty far from here. The best thing to do is to go over to Lexington Avenue and Fifty-ninth Street and take a subway up to the Bronx. You should be there in less than an hour."

"No, I'll walk. I want to see the city."

"It'll be three or four hours before you get there. Take my advice—go by subway."

"I don't mind how long it takes. I'll say the rosary."

"You're going to say lots of rosaries before you get there. Why are you so intent on going to the Bronx Zoo anyway? The Central Park Zoo is only a few blocks away."

"I live in Kenya. We have lots of big cats—lions, leopards, and cheetahs, but no tigers. The Central Park Zoo doesn't have any tigers, but the Bronx Zoo—wow! There are six of them—maybe more than any other zoo in the world."

"So in a way, you're on a quest to see a tiger."

"You could put it that way."

"I've been on my own quest of sorts. I'm looking for a store that makes the perfect chocolate egg cream."

Harbinger grimaced. "A chocolate egg cream? From the sound of it. I don't think I'd like eating one."

"It's actually a drink. It's made of milk, seltzer water, and chocolate syrup, no egg. The key to a good egg cream is the seltzer. You can't use club soda or bottled water like Perrier or Evian. It has to be old-fashioned, honest-to-God seltzer water. Sometimes I find some, but it's rare."

"I know what you mean about the right ingredients. In Lipoppo, good bean stew needs the right flavored curry, not just any curry you see in the market."

"So you can understand. We're both on quests, you to see a tiger and me to find the store that makes the perfect egg cream."

Harbinger smiled. "The secret of a quest is to never give up."

The sanitation worker thought a moment. "I get off work in about fifteen minutes. How would you like some company?"

"Company?"

"Yes, I'll walk with you to the zoo. It would be something to tell the grandchildren about. You don't get an opportunity like this very often."

"I'd love the company."

"What's your name, Father?"

"Samuel Harbinger. I'm actually a bishop."

"A bishop?"

"Yes, of Lipoppo."

"Lipoppo? Where's that?"

"In Kenya. By the way, you never told me your name."

"It's Bartholomew. Bartholomew McDermott."

"Bartholomew was one of the twelve apostles."

"Yeah, but not one of the best-known apostles."

Harbinger could only smile. "Most of us are not a Peter or a James. We are mostly all Bartholomews. "

Just then, a taxicab pulled up. The driver sounded his horn.

"There's my buddy, Tad. We usually go drinking after I get off work. I'm going to ask him to come along. He loves to do things on the spur of the moment. Is it okay to invite him?"

"Of course Tad can come."

"He probably won't walk all the way to the zoo. He goes to school in the afternoon."

"Tad's welcome to come for as long as he wants. By the way, what saint is Tad named after?"

"Thaddeus."

Bishop Harbinger smiled. "Another one of the twelve."

"I guess that's so."

* * * * * *

As the three men walked up Fifth Avenue, they saw a man lying on the ground in front of the Frick Museum at Seventieth Street. Harbinger bent over the man to see if he was injured.

"Bishop Harbinger, stay away from this derelict." Bartholomew's voice was insistent. "He could pull a knife on you."

"But he needs help, Bartholomew. He's bleeding."

"Let the police take care of him. We're never going to get to the Bronx Zoo if we try to help every down and out person in the city."

"Bartholomew, what would Jesus have us do? Pass the man by and do nothing, or stop and help him?"

Bartholomew did not answer the question.

"Tad, do you have your cell phone with you?" asked Bartholomew.

His friend looked through his pants' pockets..

"Yes, here it is."

"Where's the nearest hospital?"

"Lenox Hill. It's on Seventy-seventh Street between Park and Lexington."

Bartholomew dialed the hospital, and soon an ambulance pulled up outside the Frick Museum.

Harbinger smiled at Bartholomew. "We were lucky that Tad had one of those telephones that work without electricity."

When the ambulance had left, the three men continued up Fifth Avenue. A woman in a sequin dress and high heels walked out of Central Park, and crossing over Fifth Avenue, sauntered up to them.

"I'll make each of you a happy man for fifty dollars. Just follow me into Central Park."

Harbinger looked at the woman. "What's your name?"

"Madeline. Actually, Mary is my real name. I use Madeline professionally."

"Why are you doing this?"

"I have a daughter and that means I need money."

"Can you drive a car?" The question surprised Tad and Bartholomew.

"Yes, and I have a driver's license to prove it. Why the questions?"

"Tad, do you drive your cab every day?"

"No, only five days a week. Tuesdays and Wednesdays are my off days."

"How about letting Mary drive the cab on Tuesdays and Wednesdays—your off days?"

"You must be nuts, Bishop Harbinger. Do you really think I would let this hooker drive my car? She'd be turning tricks in the backseat in an hour."

The woman bristled. "I don't enjoy what I do. If I could get a real job, I'd grab it in a minute. Nobody wants me. I have no education; all I got is a body."

"Tad, suppose I guarantee that Mary will bring your taxi back every Wednesday? Would you let her use it then?"

"You would guarantee such a thing?"

"Yes. I'll have a bank account opened in your name, Tad."

"Where are you going to get the money, Bishop Harbinger?"

"I'll have some money after tonight."

"So, Your Excellency, you really want to go through with this?" Tad looked incredulous.

"Yes. I believe Mary won't let me down."

The woman's eyes filled up with tears. "No one has ever done such a thing for me. I promise I'll return Tad's cab—just tell me when and where."

Tad thought a moment. "Okay. I'll let her drive it on Tuesdays and Wednesdays. I'll probably rue the day, but Bishop Harbinger, you won't have to put up any money. If I can't trust a bishop of my church, who can I trust?"

Mary hugged Tad. "You won't regret this."

Bartholomew looked at his watch. "It's six o'clock. If we're going to get to the Bronx Zoo anytime today, let's get moving."

"The Bronx Zoo!" Mary giggled. "I haven't been there since I was eight years old. Mind if a hooker joins the group?"

"You can come along but only on one condition."

"What's that, Bishop?"

"You'll call yourself Mary from now on. No more Madeline!"

"Okay."

At Seventy-ninth Street, an elderly jogger broke stride to talk. "Who are you and what's your purpose?"

Harbinger answered. "We are walking to the Bronx Zoo so I can see a tiger, that's all."

"It sounds like a worthy goal to me. May I walk with you up to the Starbucks on Eighty-seventh Street? I assume you're going to stop at Starbucks?"

Bartholomew McDermott nodded. "I'm sure we will."

Just then, an off-duty police sergeant stopped to talk to Father Harbinger. "I assume no revolution is afoot, Father?"

"No. I couldn't organize a revolution if I tried."

"If you're thinking of saying an early morning Mass in Central Park, don't forget you need a permit."

"I'm not going to say Mass. My friends and I are going to the Bronx Zoo It's amazing how many people haven't been there in a long while."

"The Bronx Zoo—that's miles from here."

"I know. Why don't you come with us, Sergeant? You probably know some shortcuts."

"Which entrance are you going to?"

Father Samuel smiled. "I didn't know there was more than one."

"There are three—the main entrance at Southern Boulevard and two others—one at Fordham Road and the other at Bronxdale. I'd better go with you or you'll end up at the Bronx Botanical Gardens."

By the time they reached the Metropolitan Museum of Art at Eighty-second Street, the procession had added three more members—a waiter killing time before going to work, a night doorman on his way home, and an elderly dowager out for an early morning walk. A visit to a Starbucks on Eighty-seventh Street produced another five marchers. As the procession entered the Bronx, dozens more had joined the group. The numbers swelled into the hundreds as the crowd walked along Bronx's Grand Concourse. A news helicopter circled above the marchers.

At noon, the procession reached the Fordham Road entrance to the Bronx Zoo. Samuel Harbinger cried when he saw his first tiger. His tears were not of sadness but of joy and thanksgiving to God. He wished Banda were here.

* * * * * *

"I'm glad I came along." The police sergeant walked to where Bishop Harbinger and his three friends were standing. "You guys know how to put on a mean pilgrimage or whatever you want to call your walk."

"Thank you for helping out." Bishop Harbinger blessed the officer.

"You know, I was born here in the Bronx, right near the Grand Concourse and 170th Street. Until this morning, I haven't been back to my old neighborhood in probably ten years. Next weekend, I think I'm going to take the kids to see where Dad grew up." The sergeant brushed a tear aside. "Maybe the old lady will come, too. We're separated, but seeing where I grew up may help her to understand why I do things the way I do."

The bishop embraced the sergeant. "We say in Lipoppo that no matter where we travel, the heart never leaves the place where we were born. It will be good to bring your family here."

The officer turned to leave and then stopped. "By the way, I think you guys might be onto something—if you offered walking tours of the old neighborhoods of the city, I bet people would be lining up in droves to go on them."

The sergeant shook hands all around and hurried off to work.

Bartholomew McDermott looked at his friend Thaddeus. "Tad, that cop may be right. I bet there's a big market out there for unusual walking tours of the city. There's more to New York City than just Manhattan. I was born in Brooklyn Heights where George Washington fought the British in the American Revolution. Where did you grow up, Tad?"

"In Park Slope near Greenwood Cemetery. Lots of history is buried in there."

Mary had excitement written over her face. "I grew up in the Bronx near where Edgar Allen Poe lived—he is famous for something."

Bartholomew thought a moment. "Maybe we could put together some off-beat walking tours and see if we can make some money."

Harbinger smiled broadly. "Bartholomew, your first tour should be a search for the store that makes the best chocolate egg cream in New York."

"Bishop, what a great idea! You should become a partner with us. If you hadn't wanted to go to the Bronx Zoo, we wouldn't be here talking this way. It was you who made us see New York City in a different light."

"I can't. My life is in Africa."

Bartholomew stared at him. "Don't be so sure of that, Bishop Harbinger."

* * * * * *

That night Vincent Harbinger, the owner of The Conclave nightclub on 125th Street in Harlem, threw a gala banquet to introduce his younger brother, Samuel Harbinger, the bishop of Lipoppo, to New York's elite. The invitation to the gala mentioned four things—the location of the event (The Conclave on 125th Street), the price of admission ($15,000 for a table of ten), the nature of the attire (tails for men and appropriate formal dress for women), and a request for a contribution to The American Friends of Lipoppo for the construction of an AIDS clinic.

Every woman familiar with the New York dinner circuit knew what "appropriate formal dress," meant. Cardinal Plimpton was attending the event and sitting at the head table. Women's dresses that were red, or showed too much leg or cleavage, were to be avoided. Even with these constraints, however, women could still be daring.

Vincent Harbinger's wife Julia, for example, wore a blue-sequined gown festooned (that seemed to be the appropriate word) with a seemingly endless array of multicolored feathers. The fashion critics dubbed her, "Julia with the boa of many colors." A local politician's wife wore a beige dress printed with the faces of wild animals. Thinking that he might buy one of these dresses for Bagua, his housekeeper, the bishop made the mistake of asking the woman the price of the dress.

The woman giggled. "It costs lots at Bergdorf's." When Samuel asked his brother what "It costs lots at Bergdorf's" meant, Vincent smiled. "It probably means that the price exceeds the gross national product of some countries."

While cocktails were served, a call came in from the governor of New York asking whether there were any last-minute cancellations.

"Governor," Vincent took the call. "There is always a place at The Conclave for the chief executive of our state. Unfortunately, there's no room at the head table, but I can seat you at a table with some of my business associates."

"No offense, Vincent, but are any of your associates being investigated by the Manhattan District Attorney's Office? It's an election year and one can't be too careful."

"No."

"Then I'll take the seat."

"But one of them is being investigated by the U.S. Attorney's Office—at least that's the rumor."

The governor suddenly remembered he had another appointment.

When the guests had taken their seats, Vincent Harbinger walked up to the podium and greeted his guests.

"Seven hundred and three of my nearest and dearest friends," he began. Nobody commented on the fire department sign limiting attendance in the room to 627.

Vincent then asked Cardinal Plimpton to say grace to start the banquet. Known for his all-inclusive blessings, the cardinal thanked the farmers who grew the food, the warehousemen who stored the food, the wholesalers who brought the food to market, the cooks who prepared it, the servers who carried it to the table, and the dishwashers who ended the cycle. The only issue of drama with respect to the cardinal's blessing was whether he included wholesalers in the list of those covered by his blessing. The Catholic school system in New York City was in intermittent warfare with wholesalers about the price of food for school meals. The status of the warfare on the day of the blessing determined whether the warehousemen would be mentioned on Plimpton's list.

When the cardinal had finished his invocation, Vincent Harbinger returned to the podium. "Well, I guess the Catholic Church must have had a good day in the courts. His Eminence included warehousemen in his blessing. All kidding aside, I thank

Cardinal Plimpton for his grace. On a personal note, let me just say that the cardinal is the only man in New York who can look better in a red hat than a woman." The audience roared with laughter.

After the dinner plates were cleared from the table, Vincent Harbinger started the program of speeches.

"Now to the matter at hand. It is my distinct honor and privilege to introduce to you little bro—my younger brother, Samuel, the bishop of my birthplace, the village of Lipoppo in Kenya. For those among you who don't read the papers, watch television, or listen to the radio, I should mention that Samuel and Pope Linus were recently awarded the Nobel Peace Prize in Oslo, Norway. I should also add that my brother is here in New York to speak before the General Assembly of the United Nations. Let me turn this podium over to Samuel, but not before someone finds a Manhattan phone directory for him to stand on."

Samuel stood on the phone directory and looked out over his audience. "In my village of Lipoppo, there is an AIDS clinic. Perhaps I shouldn't call it a clinic because it is nothing more than a two-room hut with a dirt floor and six beds. It has no running water, no fans, no electric lights, not even a woolen blanket. When the rains fall, the roof leaks. When the winds blow, the patients shiver from the cold. And when they need a bedpan during the night, there is no one there to help them. This is where we bring the victims of AIDS to die.

"One day several weeks ago, a nurse sent me word to come to the clinic quickly. Six-year-old Theresa Undala was dying. The message said that her fever had spiked to one hundred and five degrees, and she barely had enough strength to lift her head off the pillow.

"When I reached the clinic, Theresa was still alive. When she saw me, she smiled. 'I was afraid you might not come, Bishop Harbinger. Remember, you promised to be here when I left to become an angel. Did you bring the sweet cakes?'

"'Yes, I even brought you the brown sugar cakes. People say they are St. Peter's favorites.'"

Theresa pulled me close. "Tell me again, Bishop Samuel, what I should do when I reach the gates of heaven. I am so excited."

"'First, find St. Peter and tell him that you've come to fill a space in the heavenly choir. Offer him the sweet cakes to let you through the gates of heaven quickly. Remember, your parents and your friends should be waiting for you just inside the gates. When you meet them, first give everybody a hug and a kiss, but don't start catching up on village gossip. There will be plenty of time to do that later. Second, go looking for Angel Gabriel. He may already have an assignment for you. You don't want to give him a bad impression by being late.'

"As I was talking to Theresa, I could see she was growing weak. Slowly, she began to slip away from me. I blessed her and anointed her with holy water. She looked at me one last time and then began her journey to God.

"When Theresa was gone, I left the clinic with tears in my eyes. I knew Theresa was in heaven. But why was she taken when she was so young? I had been taught in the seminary that God's plan for the human tace was a mystery. I wish at times like this, however, that God would lift the veil of secrecy just a little. Questioning God for not providing an explanation, however, is presumptuous. He does provide answers, but in his own time and in his own idiom.

"I come here tonight in Theresa's name and in the name of the other children of Lipoppo. They ask only that those of them who will die of this horrible disease at least be allowed to die with dignity. My brother Vincent has generously donated all the proceeds of tonight's dinner to help build a new AIDS clinic in Lipoppo.

"Others have donated money. Pope Linus contributed his half of the Nobel Peace Prize stipend to help with the construction. Cardinal Plimpton has also made a generous contribution. The archbishop of New York is a man known for his compassion. But as much as we have collected, it is not enough to build a first-class facility. I would ask you to dig deep into your pockets and make a gift for the children of my village of Lipoppo."

Vincent took the microphone from his brother's hand. "On the invitation to tonight's gala, I asked each of you to consider making a donation to build a state-of-the-art AIDS clinic in Lipoppo. I would never ask anyone to do something I wouldn't do myself."

Vincent took out his checkbook and wrote a check. "I guess you want to know the amount," he said, addressing the audience. "It's for twenty-five thousand dollars. I ask you to dig deep into your pockets and make a hefty contribution."

"Vincent, what do you suggest doing if you don't have pockets?" A woman resplendent in a black and white dress shouted from her table.

Vincent shot back. "Margie, your purse will do fine. I'm sure in the midst of all those lipsticks and powders you can find an extra five or ten thousand dollars."

"I'm no piker … here's fifteen thousand."

"Thanks, Margie, it's money well spent. Now, who else is going to help the children of Lipoppo?"

From a table near the door, an elderly dowager wobbled to her feet. "I'll help the good bishop build his clinic." She handed her sequined purse to a waiter. "Bishop Harbinger, if you look inside, you'll find a couple of hundred dollar bills. Take them. I'll send you a few more tomorrow."

Another woman stood up. "I'll also help with the clinic." She walked to the head table and handed a pearl and diamond ring to Bishop Harbinger. "It's not paste, Your Excellency. My ex-husband gave this to me. I never liked it, and I never liked him. And furthermore—cover your ears, Bishop Harbinger—my ex was not much of a lover."

The woman's humor seemed to open the floodgates of generosity. Restaurant owners wrote checks. Trucking company executives pulled wads of hundred dollar bills from their pockets.

Women removed oversize rings and necklaces and threw them into boxes being circulated through the club by waiters. Perhaps the most dramatic moment came when an anonymous donor telephoned in a gift of fifty thousand dollars.

The gift giving came to an abrupt end; however, when a woman with one champagne too many stood up and started to unzip her dress. "Take this," she shouted out. "It's too tight on me." Her escort, embarrassed by the action, whisked his date out of the club through a side door. Vincent sensed it was time for the orchestra to begin playing.

"Let me remind you all that the dancing will end promptly at two AM. Remember also—no one should try to ask the cardinal to dance, although he's not bad at Irish jigs, or so I am told."

At midnight, Vincent tallied checks and cash gifts. "I was never good at math, but if my count is right, we collected two hundred and sixty two thousand dollars tonight. Gifts of jewelry or clothing will have to be appraised before the final tally can be made."

At 12:30 AM, Cardinal Plimpton said a final grace. "God, thank you. Tonight has been Samuel Harbinger's night. A person who is a 'harbinger' is a herald—someone who announces what lies ahead. Let us hope that this man who stands before us is truly the harbinger of the future of Africa."

The applause was thunderous. The few who were there that night would not forget the emotion of that moment.

Later that night, the two brothers sat in Vincent's office.

"We have never spoken of the night our parents died, Vincent. Mobeki said they died quickly. Do you ever think of them now that you live here in New York—so far away from Lipoppo?"

"I think of them every day. How can you not think often of those you love?"

The two brothers talked and wept together until the hour grew late.

* * * * * *

The next evening, Secretary General Basil Theocritus, a widower, invited Bishop Samuel to dinner at his apartment overlooking United Nations Plaza.

"The gala last night was wonderful, Samuel. Those who attended the banquet knew exactly what was expected of them—to contribute to your AIDS clinic. Sometimes I'm afraid certain members of the United Nations have forgotten the basic reasons why they belong to the organization. My father once told me a story that illustrates the point. He was recovering from surgery and was having a hard time falling asleep. His doctor prescribed a sleeping pill for him. The first night the nurse woke my father up to give him the sleeping pill. Somehow in carrying out her specific duties, the nurse forgot the bigger picture."

Samuel laughed. "It's a good story."

"Tomorrow, there will be a vote in the Security Council over UN peacekeeping forces. The goal of these forces is to protect the people of a country by keeping warring factions apart. In many cases, however, the deployment of peacekeeping forces ends up protecting the elite but not the ordinary people. Our troops stay in relatively safe urban areas and avoid the more dangerous rural areas The vote tomorrow is about a resolution that would give me and not the Security Council as a whole, the authority to deploy peacekeeping forces."

"What are your chances of winning the vote, Mr. Secretary?"

"I'm not sure. The five permanent members of the Security Council are split. The United States wants deployment issues left with the Security Council. England supports the U.S. position, but more out of loyalty than conviction. Russia and China will vote to give me control over deployment. France—who knows what their position is! The key to all this is whether the United States will exercise its veto if it loses the vote. If the debate gets nasty, I'm sure the United States will use it. President Ableworthy can get petty when he wants to. You don't happen to have some concoction that keeps people relaxed and calm?"

"If you gave me some time, I think I could get you one."

Secretary Theocritus smiled. "I was not being serious, Samuel."

"But I was. Bagua, my housekeeper, knows how to make fragrances that will put someone to sleep, keep him awake, make him thirsty, or make him hungry."

"Yes, I have heard of this—they call it aromatherapy. Casinos release scents into the air to put people in a good mood to continue gambling."

"Basil, if aromatherapy works in an open space like a casino, there's no reason why it wouldn't work in the Security Council Chamber."

"But even if we were to use it, what scents would we use?"

"My housekeeper Bagua would know. The trick is getting in touch with her. There is only one phone in Lipoppo and it is usually busy. Zamba's wife is always talking to her daughter in Cape Town."

"Let's see if we can find your housekeeper. Call her on my land line—it's secure."

After fifteen minutes of busy signals, someone finally picked up the receiver. It was Obani, the postman.

"Obani, this is Bishop Samuel. Could you find Bagua for me? It is urgent that I speak to her."

"Yes, Bishop Samuel. At once!"

Samuel could hear Obani barking orders, and sending people to Bagua's favorite haunts. Finally, after what seemed an eternity, a familiar voice came on the line.

"Bagua, I need your advice. You once told me that the glands of a giraffe let off a smell that puts people to sleep. Do you know something that would relax people but keep them awake?"

"That's easy. Mix lavender, skullcap, chamomile, and kingombo in eucalyptus oil. The smell will relax an elephant."

"What's kingombo in English, Bagua?"

"I don't know. I've always called it kingombo. Hold on. Let me ask Miriam—she'll know."

Five minutes later, an out-of-breath Bagua returned to the phone. "It's called okra."

"Okra? Are you sure, Bagua?"

"That's what Miriam says. Mix okra in with the other ingredients and you'll see results."

"Thank you, Bagua."

Harbinger hung up the phone.

"Mr. Secretary, you heard what we need: chamomile, skullcap, lavender, eucalyptus oil, and okra."

"Samuel, let's go out and buy what we need. I know the place to start—Paldocci's in Greenwich Village."

* * * * * *

The secretary general's limousine double-parked outside the food store. Eucalyptus oil and lavender took only minutes to find. After rummaging around shelves, a helpful grocery clerk was able to discover chamomile and skullcap. To find okra, however, the store manager had to help with the search. He telephoned other food markets throughout Manhattan but without any success. Throwing up his hands in frustration, the manager summarized the situation. "I'm afraid that tonight New York City is a metropolis without okra. I can get you some by tomorrow night but that's the best I can do."

The secretary general shook his head. "Unfortunately, that will be too late."

"Let me call Bagua back, Secretary General. There must be another ingredient we can substitute for okra."

Theocritis handed his cell phone to Harbinger. "Remember this line is not secure, Samuel"

"If anyone wants to eavesdrop, I hope they will enjoy the talk about okra substitutes, Mr. Secretary General."

* * * * * *

Harbinger dialed Lipoppoo over and over again only to be

met by busy signals.. "I'm going to have to speak to Zamba's wife about the amount of time she spends on the phone. Basil, isn't there some other way to reach Bagua?"

"There's a United Nations office in Nairobi. I'll have a helicopter sent to Lipoppo to find your housekeeper. We should be able to get an answer in a couple of hours.".

* * * * * *

"Bagua says to try eggplant in place of okra. She thinks it will work, but she's never actually made the recipe without okra."

"Well, the vote's tomorrow. I have no choice. I'll send my driver down to the all-night market to pick up eggplant. Did Bagua say how much we need?"

"No. Tell your driver to buy several pounds of it. There's an African saying, 'It's easier to deal with too much than with too little.'"

* * * * * *

Gilbert Cleverhand, the United States secretary of state, asked for a meeting with the president.

"The secretary general put in a call to a United Nations office in Nairobi, Mr. President..He asked for a helicopter to fly to a village called Lipoppo and speak to a woman named Bagua about okra.."

"About what?"

"Okra!"

"You can't be serious, Mr. Secretary."

"The word must be code for something. We think the letters mean 'Okay, resign alternative.'"

"It could refer to tomorrow's vote in the Security Council on deployment of peacekeeping forces. Maybe Theocritus will resign if he loses the vote. I don't want that. As bad as he is, there could be worse. Tell our ambassador at the UN to vote 'no' on the resolution, but if we lose the vote, don't exercise our veto."

160

"Yes, Mr. President."

* * * * * *

At about midnight, the secretary general's driver arrived back with four bags of eggplant.

"I bought all the eggplant the market had. If you wish, I'll see if some other markets are open."

The secretary general patted his driver's shoulder reassuringly. "You've bought more than enough."

The ingredients were spread out on the kitchen table. Bishop Harbinger poured the eucalyptus oil into a large bowl. The secretary general then added chamomile, lavender, and skullcap. When it came time to add the eggplant, Samuel placed three of them in a blender. In a minute, the eggplant turned into paste. With a spoon, Secretary Theocritus scooped the paste from the blender and dropped it into the bowl.

"I feel like an alchemist mixing a secret potion in order to achieve some forbidden purpose."

"I think I feel the same as you, Mr. Secretary, but I can't be sure."

"Why not?"

"What's an alchemist?"

"In your country, you would probably call him a medicine man or a shaman."

"Well, then I do feel like this alchemist of yours."

In a matter of minutes, a pungent, licorice-like aroma filled the room. Samuel Harbinger started to hum and swirl around the secretary general's kitchen table.

"I haven't felt this happy since the day I was ordained a priest."

"Do you know, Samuel?" The secretary general had a silly grin on his face. "I almost don't care who wins the vote tomorrow. Bagua should be awarded the Nobel Prize for Chemistry."

After taking another inhale of the potion, the secretary general pushed a buzzer at his desk and Security Officer Becu answered.

"Becu, it will be hot in the Security Council's Chamber tomorrow. I'm going to put some air freshener in the room. Stop by in the morning to pick it up."

* * * * * *

The secretary general couldn't believe what he was hearing. One after another, the members of the Security Council voted him the sole authority to deploy UN peacekeeping forces. When it was over, the tally was fifteen to zero with the United States casting a last minute yes vote.

As they filed out of the Security Council Chamber, the secretary was amazed to see delegates laughing and walking arm and arm with one another. A delegate from Germany, a rather dour-looking gentleman from Hanover, whistled Beethoven's Ninth Symphony as he left the chamber. It was the conduct of the delegate from the People's Republic of China; however, that most surprised the secretary general. The man actually smiled. After working with the Chinese delegate for three years, the secretary general believed the delegate lacked the musculature needed to show his teeth.

The last person to leave the Security Council Chamber was the delegate from Argentina, a flirtatious woman whose skirts were always provocative. She made a noisy spectacle of gathering her papers before finally walking out the door. When the chamber was finally empty, the secretary general telephoned Bishop Harbinger.

"The aromatherapy worked, Samuel. The Security Council voted to give my office the power to deploy UN peacekeeping forces. Miracle of miracles, in the end, even the United States voted for the resolution. If anything, Bagua's concoction might have been a little stronger than necessary. If I'm not mistaken, the delegate from Argentina was trying to seduce me."

"I will call Bagua and tell her the good news. She can bottle the mix and sell it in Nairobi."

The secretary was in a playful mood. "I think your Bagua should stick to using okra."

That night the two men toasted Bagua. The secretary provided a bottle of his finest French wine. Bishop Harbinger drank only half a glass.

Late that night, the Argentine delegate called to see whether the secretary general was aware of some recent developments in the Falkland Islands. She volunteered to come to Secretary Theocritus' apartment to give him a briefing.

The secretary general demurred, citing a headache.

"Samuel, tell Bagua that she should most definitely stick to okra."

* * * * * *

The president phoned his secretary of state. "Gilbert, I thought we had agreed to vote 'no' on the resolution. Why did our ambassador vote in favor of it?"

"He said he got carried away, Mr. President. The only thing I can say in his defense is that the press has been giving us high marks for our 'yes' vote."

* * * * * *

Bishop Harbinger's speech to the General Assembly was only hours away. He walked into St. Patrick's Cathedral and sat in a back pew. Harbinger thought of his beloved village of Lipoppo and of Bagua, Obani, and his many friends there. As he watched the crowds go in and out of the cathedral, his mind kept coming back to Bagua and the cookies she had sent to Secretary General Theocritus. Suddenly, Samuel Harbinger stood up from the pew, left the cathedral, and walked toward the United Nations building. He knew what he would say.

* * * * * *

"Ladies and Gentlemen, it is my pleasure to introduce to you Samuel Harbinger, the Bishop of Lipoppo in Kenya." The secretary general stood at the rostrum facing a packed General Assembly Chamber. "Many of us who work in the public arena often forget our values and sometimes even our integrity. We say we labor to help the poor and the disadvantaged, only to find ourselves doing them more harm than good. I have asked Bishop Harbinger to address the General Assembly today because he is that rare exception—a simple and uncomplicated man, a man who sees God in the sunrise and in the sunset, and a man who has compassion for all of God's creation."

When the applause had ended, Samuel Harbinger stood alone at the rostrum.

"In my village in Kenya, we have a wonderful custom. Before we begin our Council of Elders' meetings, Hestern, the carpenter, calls out the names of council members who have died. The rest of us answer 'present.' We recognize that those who have gone before us are still present in our lives. They animate our decisions today as they did yesterday.

"Let me recite the names of those who have led the United Nations, and let me ask all of you to answer 'present.' Calling out their names reminds us of their presence among us.

Harbinger picked up the list of prior secretary generals.

"Secretary General Trygve Lie."

There was an awkward silence until the delegate from Norway stood up from his chair and shouted out. "My fellow countryman Secretary General Trygve Lie is present."

"Dag Hammarskjöld."

Hundreds in the audience leapt to their feet and cried out "present."

"U Thant."

The chamber erupted in shouts of "present."

"Kurt Waldheim."

Although some in the room remained silent because of the

secretary general's political leanings during World War II, the word "present" reverberated around the crowded chamber.

"Javier Perez de Cuellar."

Many who stood and cried "present" remembered the elegant Peruvian with great fondness and affection.

"Boutros Boutros-Ghali."

The cries of "present" were deafening.

"Kofi Annan." Many stood in tears and shouted "here."

"Ban Ki-Moon." The South Korean delegation cried out "present."

Few who were there in the General Assembly Chamber would forget the emotion of that moment. When Bishop Samuel finished the roll call of past secretaries general, he waited at the podium until the delegates and invited guests returned to their seats.

"A week ago when I arrived at the airport, I brought with me a gift for Secretary General Theocritus. It was a gift, which my housekeeper, Bagua, had made. It was a platter of cookies, one for each member state in the United Nations—one hundred and ninety-two cookies in all. Bagua cannot read or write, but with the help of her nine-year-old daughter, she printed the name of a nation on each cookie. It took days for them to do it. Then in an instant, the gift was gone. As it was carried off the plane, the platter fell down the steps of the ramp. Most of the cookies broke in half. Symbolically, the United Nations lay in pieces on the ground."

Samuel Harbinger glanced at the VIP seating but did not see Cardinal Plimpton among the invited guests.

"Secretary Theocritus asked me to speak to you today but gave me no topic. Somehow, the picture of Bagua's cookies lying broken on the ground kept coming back to me. So I thought I would speak to you about my housekeeper, Bagua, and her simple gift to the United Nations.

"A teacher once posed a question to his students. 'When does darkness turn to light?' Each student shouted out an answer. One shouted, 'When you can see that a horse is not a zebra'; another,

'When you can see that an apple tree is not a cherry tree'; a third, 'When you can see that a man is not a woman.' The teacher shook his head at each answer. Finally, one student asked the teacher to tell them the answer to his question. 'Darkness turns to light,' the teacher replied, 'when you can see in the face of a stranger the face of your brother or your sister.' Bagua could be that teacher. She always brings the stranger into her house and gives him food and drink. To her there is no Zulu or Tutsi or Yoruba, there is only a man or a woman created by God in his own image." Bishop Harbinger paused a moment. His eyes welled with tears.

"If I were to tell Bagua that her gift to Secretary Theocritus lay in broken batches on the ground, she would shed no tear. Instead, she would praise God for the chance to make a gift for so important a person as the secretary general of the United Nations. The meek shall inherit the earth, reads the Christian scripture. Bagua and all the people like her in this world—the farmer in China, the sheepherder in Australia, the seamstress in Hong Kong, the fisherman in Japan, the wood carver in Kenya—they are those for whom this organization exists." His voice quavering, Bishop Harbinger struggled to finish his speech. "You must never forget that."

Suddenly, a security officer opened the entrance door to the General Assembly Chamber. Cardinal Plimpton walked into the hushed amphitheater carrying a platter of cookies.

"I had asked my housekeeper to bake these for Secretary Theocritus. She spoke to Bagua to get the recipe."

The chamber erupted in applause as he handed the tray of cookies to the secretary general.

* * * * * *

Outside the United Nations building, life went on much as usual.

A woman stood at Forty-seventh Street and First Avenue trying to hail a taxicab.

A student headed across Forty-second Street to the New York Public Library.

An attendant, resplendent in black hat and burgundy coat, welcomed guests to the Millenium UN Plaza Hotel.

"Let me take your luggage, sir. Yes, that building across the street is the United Nations. They are having a special session today. An African bishop from a village called Lipoppo is addressing the General Assembly. Most unusual choice for a speaker, don't you think?"

Chapter Ten
An Unexpected Visitor

Obani, the postman, was just finishing his deliveries when a limousine drove into Lipoppo. Curious about who had come to the village, Obani watched as the driver parked the limousine in front of the bank. Perrier bottle in hand, a tall man elegantly dressed in a blue pinstriped suit and dark maroon tie stepped out of the car and walked to where Obani stood.

"Sir, is this the village of Lipoppo? There is no sign on the road."

"Yes. This is Lipoppo."

"I am looking for Bishop Samuel Harbinger."

"The bishop lives here. What is your name?"

"Francis Baellert, dean of the Harvard University Graduate School. Could you take me to him?"

"Bishop Samuel is scrimmaging with the fifth grade soccer team."

"Where is the soccer field? I'll watch the game until it's over."

Obani could see that Baellert was perspiring from the heat and humidity. "There is no shade there at this time of day."

"My car is air-conditioned. I'll manage."

"The soccer field is about a kilometer down the road. If you wish, I will take you there."

"Thank you. Tell the driver where to go and he'll drive us."

"You said you are a dean of a university called Harvard. I think I've heard of your school. It is in Washington, DC. Many Africans have gone to school there."

"No, that is Howard University, not Harvard."

"Does your university have African students?"

"Of course, we do."

Suddenly, a soccer ball bounced across the road. Within seconds, a swarm of children came chasing after it. The driver slammed on the brakes narrowly missing one of the players.

Obani jumped out of the limousine. "Bishop Samuel, are you all right?"

"Yes, but I wish I'd gotten to the ball before it went out of bounds. I would have had a clear shot at the goal."

"Bishop, you have a guest," said Obani. "He comes from Harvard University in the United States."

Francis Baellert got out of the limousine and shook hands with the bishop.

"Your Excellency, you met the president of Harvard, John Wedgwood, briefly in Oslo at the Nobel Peace Prize reception. Since I was traveling to Africa on university business, President Wedgwood asked that I bring you a personal message from the Board of Overseers of the university. I tried to call you before I drove out from Nairobi, but the telephone was always busy."

"I'm sorry. We only have one phone in Lipoppo and Zamba's wife is always using it. Her daughter in Cape Town just had a baby and she must call five times a day to see how her grandchild is doing. The village elders have told her unless she stops, she will have to install her own phone line. But she pays them no attention. She is stubborn."

"No matter. We've finally made contact. That's the important thing."

"Mr. Baellert, I must finish the soccer game or the fifth grade class will be disappointed. We can talk at the rectory when the game is over."

Bishop Samuel threw the ball back into play and disappeared into the resulting fracas.

* * * * * *

An hour later, Bishop Harbinger and his guest sat at the dining room table in the rectory. The bishop's housekeeper, Bagua, scurried about the kitchen warming tea and baking pastries for their unexpected visitor.

"I am flattered that someone from Harvard University would travel all the way out to Lipoppo to see me."

"There's a reason for the visit." Baellert neatened a pile of paperclips in a china bowl on the table. "The Board of Overseers of the university has voted unanimously to award you an honorary degree of Doctor of Laws at this year's commencement exercises."

A confused look passed over the bishop's face. "What is an honorary degree?"

"Don't be fooled by the word 'honorary'—it's a Harvard degree like any other. It's given to someone who has made a significant contribution to humanity."

"Who else has received this honorary degree from your university?"

"Albert Einstein, Winston Churchill, and Mother Teresa all have received honorary degrees from Harvard."

"I do not deserve to be ranked with such people."

"Let Harvard be the judge of that. You won the Nobel Peace Prize. Nobel laureates have an aura about them."

"I have been told that there is fierce competition among

universities to have the largest number of Nobel laureates. Laureates increase donations."

"There is no question that the number of Nobel laureates increases the prestige of a university. Increased prestige leads to increased donations, but it also leads to better students and faculty. Harvard wants to start building a relationship with you. We hope you will accept our honorary degree as a first step. Maybe someday you'll join the faculty in our Divinity School or in one of our graduate departments. We would hope to award you the honorary degree at this year's commencement. Of course, you would be expected to give the commencement address to the graduates."

"What day is your commencement?"

"June ninth."

Harbinger thought a moment. He pulled out a tattered pocket calendar and looked at it. "I'm sorry, Mr. Baellert. I have a conflict. June ninth is Lipoppo's elementary school graduation. Lately, I have been away so much from the village that I should not miss it."

Baellert looked startled. "You would turn down a Harvard honorary degree to be at a village elementary school graduation?"

"It is not just any elementary school graduation—it is Lipoppo's elementary school graduation. I am their bishop. Bagua's daughter and Hestern's son are graduating.

Baellert shrugged. "Bishop Harbinger, I admire your sense of obligation. It is refreshing to see it practiced rather than simply talked about. Would you accept the degree if we conferred it on a different date—say in mid-May? Harvard has awarded an honorary degree 'out of season' before."

"Out of season?"

Baellert laughed. "That's Harvard way of saying an honorary degree that is not awarded at commencement but at a special convocation."

"Who has received one of these honorary degrees out of season?"

"George Washington in 1776, Winston Churchill in 1943, and Nelson Mandela in 1998. If the overseers approve granting the degree at a special convocation, could you come to Harvard on May fifteenth?"

Harbinger looked again at his pocket calendar. "Yes, I could come on that day. If I were to accept, would I still be expected to give a speech?"

"Yes. There would be a full academic procession, the conferring of the honorary degree, and then your remarks. We will invite our alumni and interested students. I should mention one more thing. Once you are awarded the degree, you will be entitled to all the privileges of a Harvard faculty member—the use of the faculty club and all athletic facilities, online access to the Widener Library, discounts at the Harvard Coop for all book and clothing purchases. And there's one more perk—free on-campus parking."

"But I cannot drive an automobile."

"Then I will have to teach you. It will be my personal gift to a friend."

"Obani tried to teach me first in the village Jeep and then again in the Range Rover. He finally gave up. He says that I am not equipped for the world of technology."

Baellert roared with laughter. "To use the idiom of the day, you are technologically challenged. I'm sure I'll be able to teach you. When I was in graduate school, I worked part time as a driving instructor. My students all passed the driving test. You will, too."

"You've convinced me, Dean Baellert. I accept."

"Give me a moment to check with President Wedgwood just to be sure the overseers will agree to award the degree at a special convocation on May fifteenth."

Baellert took his cell phone and stepped outside the rectory.

He returned in five minutes. "President Wedgwood says 'yes' to the May fifteenth convocation. And now for the bonus."

"The bonus?"

"Yes. If you accepted our honorary degree, the Board of Overseers authorized me to award scholarships to two students from Lipoppo. The university will pay tuition, travel, and all living expenses. The semester begins two weeks from today."

Bishop Harbinger hugged the Harvard dean. "This is a great honor for Lipoppo. I will ask the Council of Elders to select the two students next week. Thank the Board of Overseers for their generosity to our village."

"Good. Now if our business is complete, could I prevail on you for a tour of the countryside. I've never been in this part of Africa before. My driver will take us."

"It would be better if we went by bicycle."

"Your Excellency, can I share a dark secret with you?"

"Of course."

"I never learned to ride a bike. I was an only child, and my parents were a bit overprotective. My mother kept worrying that I would fall off the bicycle and scrape my knees."

"Well, since you've volunteered to teach me to drive, I'll teach you to ride a bicycle. But first I have to ask you a question."

"What?"

"Do you face problems head on or are you more cautious and hesitant? Learning to ride a bicycle has a lot to do with a person's attitude toward life."

"I guess I'm a bit on the cautious side."

"Well, you must learn to trust in yourself. If you do, in a couple of hours you'll be pedaling around Lipoppo as if you've been doing it all your life."

Dean Baellert laughed. "Just make sure if I fall, I fall into tall grass."

"I promise no scraped knees."

True to his word, Samuel Harbinger had Baellert up on his bike within an hour, and braking within an hour more. After mastering several pointers on steering and after some final wobbling, Samuel Harbinger declared Baellert ready to take a bicycle tour of the countryside.

As the two men pedaled out of Lipoppo, Samuel Harbinger pointed to a woman hurrying along the road.

"There goes Zamba's wife on her way to the post office. She's probably made three calls to Cape Town already today."

* * * * * *

The process of selecting which students would go to Harvard University consumed the attention of the village of Lipoppo for the better part of a week. The Council of Elders interviewed all children between the ages of sixteen and twenty.

Their first choice was Martha, the banker's daughter. Martha, a quiet seventeen-year-old, was a voracious reader. According to her teacher, she had read every book in the village library and had committed to memory long passages from many of them. Martha particularly impressed the Council of Elders with her recitation of the first chapters of the book of Genesis.

Martha's selection, however, was almost derailed by her pet cheetah cub. She had tamed the animal and insisted on taking it to Harvard. No amount of persuasion by her father Nelson could change her mind. Bishop Harbinger finally asked to speak with her.

"Martha, at Harvard, students live in buildings called dormitories. Each student is assigned a roommate. What if your roommate is afraid of the cheetah or complains to the school authorities? And what happens when there is ice and snow? Cheetahs are not used to the cold. Your cub may become sick."

Bishop Harbinger's intervention had the desired effect. The next day, Martha agreed to go to Harvard by herself as long as her father would let the cub live in their family home. Martha's father readily agreed.

The second choice by the Council of Elders was another

seventeen-year-old—Mark, the son of Ningoro, the village cobbler. At the age of six, Mark began to carve wooden statues of animals. His lions and giraffes brought a good price in Nairobi. With Bishop Harbinger's encouragement, Mark started to carve African nativity scenes—Mary, Joseph, and the newborn Jesus surrounded by the animals of the water hole. In time, Mark added to the nativity scene the Three Wise Men and their camels. So popular did these African crèche sets become that Mark trained other children in the village to help with the carvings.

Mark possessed one other talent that persuaded the elders to send him to Harvard. The boy was born fast—at least that's how his father Ningoro put it. Tall and slim, Mark could outrun anyone in Lipoppo or in the neighboring village of Woomba. As he grew older, the boy imagined himself winning a gold medal in the Olympic Games. When he was fourteen, Mark's father took his son to Nairobi to compete for a berth on Kenya's Olympic track team. Although he won the 800-meter race by a wide margin, Mark was denied a place on the team. For the public record, the coach thought him too young. Mark's father, however, believed that the coach had been bribed to select the runner-up.

Having made its selections, the Council of Elders now faced the issue of supervision. By a vote of nine to one, the elders asked Bishop Harbinger to accompany the students to Harvard.

"Mark and Martha have never left Kenya," the head of the council said to Harbinger. "They will not understand how to use a credit card, tip in a restaurant, or dress for the cold weather."

Given the nine to one vote, and the fact that the one negative vote was his own, Harbinger reluctantly acceded to the wishes of the council, and he agreed to accompany Mark and Martha to Boston. He would stay at Harvard for two weeks. No more, he told the council.

* * * * * *

United Airlines Flight 403 landed at Logan International

Airport in a blizzard. The plane sat for two hours on the runway before it could taxi to its assigned gate. When the passengers were finally allowed to disembark, Bishop Harbinger helped Mark and Martha gather their belongings from the overhead compartments on the plane.

As they exited the Boeing 747, a tall man bundled in a wool overcoat and fur hat walked up to them.

"I presume the contingent from Lipoppo has arrived in Boston!"

Bishop Harbinger burst into laughter. "Francis, I didn't recognize you under all your clothes." The two men hugged.

"Samuel, I didn't expect to see you until May fifteenth."

"The Council of Elders asked that I accompany Mark and Martha to Harvard. I'm here for two weeks only."

A young man in his early twenties stood next to Baellert.

"Dad, would you introduce me to our guests?"

"Sorry. Let me introduce my son, Sean. He has brought the three of you something."

Sean Baellert bent down and opened a suitcase. "I thought you'd be cold, so I ransacked my closet for coats, sweaters, scarves, and stocking hats. I even brought along a pair of ski pants."

Five minutes later, Bishop Harbinger, Mark, and Martha, dressed in an odd assortment of woolen outfits, made their way toward the door of the terminal building.

As Sean Baellert pushed open the door, Martha suddenly began to tremble. She tried to run back inside the building but Bishop Harbinger stopped her.

"What's wrong, Martha?" Samuel Harbinger put his arms around her.

"White smoke is coming out of my mouth. Bishop Samuel, please take me home. I do not wish to go to this Harvard place."

The bishop smiled. "Martha, the smoke is caused by cold weather. It will not harm you."

"Please take me back to Lipoppo. I don't like this cold weather."

Sean pointed across the concourse. "Do you see that store, Martha? It is called McDonald's. You can buy things there that will make you feel better. Let me get you a Big Mac and a chocolate shake and see how you feel then."

"Will this Big Mac make the white smoke go away?"

"Not exactly, but I think you may reconsider staying in Boston after you taste it."

Baellert and Harbinger waited while Sean took Mark and Martha over to McDonald's.

"Remember, Samuel, I owe you driving lessons. If we start tomorrow, we should be finishing parallel parking about the time you have to go back to Lipoppo. You can take the driving test when you come back for your honorary degree."

"What time tomorrow, Francis?"

"Suppose I come by the Harvard Club tomorrow morning at ten o'clock. Is that too early?"

"No."

"After the lesson, we will swing by the president's office for a brief hello. President Wedgwood looks forward to seeing you again. He enjoyed meeting you in Oslo. By the way, the president would like Mark and Martha to come to his office as well."

* * * * * *

Promptly at 10:00 AM, there was a loud knock on the door of Harbinger's room at the Harvard Club.

"Samuel, are you in there?"

"Yes, Francis." Bishop Harbinger threw on a cassock and opened the door.

"Okay, let's go. You'll be driving before you know it."

"I hope so. But shouldn't we postpone today's lesson because of the snow last night?"

"The snow has already been cleared. The first decision you must make is whether you want to learn on a stick or on an automatic. I recommend an automatic."

"That would be fine."

"Any special requests before we get started?"

"Special requests?"

"Yes. Like a rabbit tail for the windshield or a plastic St. Christopher for the dashboard. When you get your license, you can get a St. Otto—he's the patron saint of parking spaces."

Bishop Harbinger laughed. "I'll pass on the saints and the rabbit tail. But maybe I should get glasses before I begin."

"Are you nearsighted or farsighted?"

"I can't see objects far away."

"Then you're nearsighted."

"I don't understand. If I can't see objects that are far away, why am I called nearsighted?"

"Because you can see things up close. We'll have to buy you glasses. You have to be able to read signs if you're going to find your way around the city. By the way, are you astigmatic?"

Harbinger was startled by the question.

"I am in communion with Rome, Francis. I am not a schismatic."

Baellert laughed. "I asked if you were astigmatic, not whether you were a schismatic."

Harbinger held up his hands for Baellert to see.

"I'm not a stigmatic, either, Francis. I do not have the five wounds of Jesus."

"Let's forget astigmatism for the moment. What about color blindness?"

"What do you mean by color blindness?"

"Tell me what color sweater I'm wearing."

"It's green."

"I think you were right, Samuel. We should postpone your first driving lesson."

"Why?"

"First, Samuel, my sweater is gold, not green. I think you are color-blind."

"And?"

"Second, even though you do not want a plastic St. Christopher for the dashboard, I think I should get one."

* * * * * *

President Wedgwood stood up from his desk and walked across the room to greet his guests.

"Samuel, I'm glad you accepted our honorary degree of Doctor of Laws."

"Thank you."

"I understand that Dean Baellert gave you your first driving lesson this morning. How did he do, Francis?"

"I can't comment on that. Isn't there a driving instructor–student privilege?"

"What Francis is really saying, President Wedgwood, is that there were some technical difficulties that required a postponement."

"Well, I'm sure Francis will reschedule it. And these two handsome teenagers must be Mark and Martha. Welcome to Harvard. I have arranged for you to meet Felice Fergusine, our career counselor for African students. She'll help you outline a curriculum for your freshman year."

Mark nervously handed the president a brown paper bag.

"What's this, Mark?"

"I carved it for you, sir."

Inside the bag was one of Mark's nativity sets.

"This is beautiful, Mark."

"I put you in as one of the magi, President Wedgwood."

Wedgwood guffawed. "I wonder how many of the faculty would agree that I was one of the wise men. Thank you, Mark. It will go in a place of honor in my home."

* * * * * *

Felice Fergusine, Harvard's career counselor for African students, greeted Mark and Martha at the door to her office. All forms of African beadwork cluttered Fergusine's desk. On the walls hung carvings of Masai warriors. A pair of Zulu spears stood in the corner.

"The two of you come on in. Take off your coats and make yourselves at home."

"Thank you for seeing us," said Martha.

"The president's office asked me to map out a curricular plan for your first year at Harvard. Let me begin with you, Mark."

Fergusine picked up a file marked Lipoppo—Top Priority—Presidential Interest.

"Mark, I'm going to suggest a straight liberal arts curriculum for you. Nothing too practical. We're going to think long term."

"Long term?"

"Yes, very long term—thirty years from now—when you are a leader in the new Africa."

"Okay. At least I guess so."

"For a science course, I recommend The Phenomenology of Trauma. The title speaks for itself. As for a literature offering, you are a fortunate young man, Mark. This semester Professor Kermel is teaching her course on early Jane Austen. It doesn't get a big enrollment, but I think you would enjoy it. An Introduction to Pure Math is always a good course to take so let's add that to your schedule. Then Professor Crotty, chair of the Art History Department, is teaching a course entitled, Shaker Cupboards in Eighteenth-Century Vermont. Given your interest in woodcarving, Mark, you should take the course."

"You think I should take a course in eighteenth-century shaker cupboards?"

"Yes. By the way, your personalized nativity scenes have caused a sensation on the campus. President Wedgwood happened to show your handiwork to some friends and now everybody wants one. In fact, could I put in an order for one?"

"Sure. What figure would you like to be—an angel, a shepherd, or maybe the owner of the inn? I am thinking of introducing a new figure—a woman who offers Mary the swaddling clothes to wrap around the newborn baby."

"Could I be one of the magi?"

"The first woman wise man?"

"Yes."

"I don't think so. The scriptures say the magi were all men. I don't want to change the basic story line."

"Well then, the innkeeper would be okay."

"You can be either a short or a tall innkeeper."

"A tall one."

"One more question. Do you want to have straight or curly hair?"

"Curly hair."

"Okay, you will be my first tall, curly haired innkeeper."

Smiling, Fergusine picked up the Lipoppo file again. "Now, Martha, let's look at you. Like Mark, we're going to go the liberal arts route. I recommend Sanskrit as a good language course."

"Are there any people who speak Sanskrit?"

"No, but so what? It's the root of many of the Indo-Aryan languages."

"Which languages are they?"

"Nepali, Hindi, Bengali—and there are many more."

"I think I would rather take Hindi, which some people speak rather than Sanskrit which nobody speaks."

"Before discussing my language choice in isolation, Martha, let's look at the rest of the curriculum I'm proposing. It's an integrated whole."

"Okay."

"For your math course, I would recommend the same course I recommended for Mark—An Introduction to Pure Math. I think a good literature course for you, Martha, would be Early Chaucer."

"Who's he?"

"A medieval poet."

"What kind of poet is a medieval poet?"

"He's a poet who wrote during the Middle Ages."

"And what science offering should I take? Maybe there is a course that studies cattle or sheep?"

"We do not teach animal husbandry here at Harvard. I suggest you take Migratory Patterns of the Mexican Spotted Owl. Now do you see the integrated whole I'm suggesting for you? Sanskrit is a better pick than Hindi."

"No, Ms. Fergusine. I don't see it—the integrated whole, that is. I don't want to take a course in Sanskrit or frankly in Hindi, either. I'd like to take a course in German. I met a man once who spoke it."

"German! Over Sanskrit and Hindi?"

"Yes. And Mark and I have a suggestion. Both of us want to take a course in business. We wanted to start a company that sells Mark's nativity scenes here in Boston. Mark would do the carving, and I would do the publicity and collect the money."

"This is all quite unorthodox—taking a course in business. It's not liberal arts."

"We realize that Harvard has given us money to come here to learn. Mark and I appreciate that. But this liberal arts stuff is not what we want to study."

"This is most unorthodox."

"You said that before, Ms. Fergusine. Does that mean you are saying 'yes' to a business course?"

"There is an offering called Entrepreneurship. It teaches you how to start a small business. I guess I could enroll both of you in it."

"That would be great, Ms. Fergusine. And there are a couple of other courses that Mark and I would like to discuss with you."

"Which ones?"

"The courses on early Jane Austen and early Chaucer."

* * * * * *

The next morning, a bleary-eyed Samuel Harbinger sat on his

bicycle outside Dean Baellert's house just off the Harvard campus. At five AM, Francis Baellert opened the garage door and wheeled his bike over to where Harbinger was waiting.

"It's pretty cold this morning, Samuel. Before we take off, come in for some coffee and eggs. Sean is cooking."

"Okay. Some coffee would be great."

After breakfast, the two men got on their bicycles. Harbinger stopped for a minute to adjust his handelbars.

"Is there a problem, Samuel?"

"No but I always check the handlebars. I had an accident once."

"Tell me what happened."

"It involved a lioness who was having infidelity concerns. I'll tell you the story when it's a bit warmer."

"By the way, I hear your students gave Felice Fergusine an earful yesterday."

"What did they say?"

"They challenged the benefits of a liberal arts curriculum. They supposedly called it 'this liberal arts stuff.' Everybody is talking about it."

"Harvard has been incredibly generous to Mark and Martha. I hope their comment is not interpreted as ingratitude"

"Not at all, Samuel. It's good to hear someone challenge the accepted orthodoxy . Somehow I think Harvard will weather the storm and live to fight another day." Baellert put on his woolen gloves. "Well, Samuel, what's our destination for this morning's bike ride?"

"Let's go to the Charles River."

"It'll be frozen over."

Harbinger's eyes opened wide. "I've never seen such a thing in Kenya."

"Well then, let's go." Pulling stocking caps down over their ears, the two men pedaled across the Harvard campus. A blustery wind forecast snow later in the day.

When the two friends reached the bank of the Charles River, they stopped. "Let's ride out on the ice, Francis."

"Samuel, I'm not sure it's thick enough."

"Well, let's see." Harbinger pedaled out on the ice. "C'mon, Francis. See, it won't crack."

"Well I'm not going to take the chance, Samuel.. I'm heavier than you are and I can't swim,"

" Just do it, Francis. I promise you won't have to swim and you won't scrape your knees."

"Okay."Baellert closed his eyes, and taking a deep breath, followed Samuel Harbinger out onto the ice.

Harbinger cheered. "Francis, look around you. You've never seen Harvard from quite this angle before. We're like explorers seeing a new world for the first time."

And so, scarves blowing out behind them, Francis Baellert, dean of Harvard University's Graduate School, and Samuel Harbinger, Bishop of Lipoppo, Kenya, rode across the frozen Charles River.

* * * * * *

"This is your Captain speaking." The Egypt Air flight began its final approach to Nairobi Airport. "We have managed to keep ahead of the rain, but I'm afraid it's caught up with us now. Tighten your seat belts and prepare for a bit of a bumpy landing. Other than that, let me welcome you to Nairobi."

Harbinger's two weeks at Harvard were over. Despite the foul weather, Bishop Harbinger was glad to be coming home to Kenya. He missed his friends.

When the jet hit the runway, the captain threw the engines into reverse. The plane rattled and shook until it skidded to a halt at the far end of the runway.

The captain came into the cabin. The passengers broke into applause. "Well, that really wasn't so bad, folks. See you on another Egypt Air flight soon."

* * * * * *

After Harbinger picked up his luggage from the conveyor belt, he went in search of Nelson and the village Range Rover. Usually, Nelson would sit double-parked just to the right of the Egypt Air claims area. But not today. Harbinger ducked under an awning to keep dry while he waited for Nelson to arrive. Suddenly he heard a horn honking and saw the Range Rover inching its way toward him. He was surprised to see Father Albert behind the wheel.

"Sorry I'm late, Samuel. With the rains, all the roads are muddy and some are impassable."

"I wasn't expecting you, Albert. Nelson usually picks me up."

"We thought it would be better if I came this time."

"There is something wrong, Albert. What is it?"

"I don't know how to tell you this."

"Tell me what, Albert? Has Banda not stayed east of the tree line and been shot?"

"No, he's fine."

"Does it have anything to do with building the AIDS clinic?"

"No, the foreman of the project told Obani that with the stipend from the Nobel Peace Prize, there is enough money to begin construction."

"Then what's the problem, my good friend?"

Father Albert took a deep breath.

"I'm leaving the priesthood, Samuel."

"Don't joke with me, Albert."

"I'm not joking."

"Why, Albert?"

"I have met a woman. She makes me feel like a man again."

"But what about your vows?"

"If God is a caring God, as we believe him to be, then he will understand. I have tried to stay a priest. I have thought of little else over these past few months."

"What will you do?"

185

"Lacata and I will leave Woomba tomorrow night. A friend will drive us back here to Nairobi to catch a flight to London. Lacata has a cousin there."

"You must leave so soon?"

"Yes. My housekeeper, Yobate, says there are already rumors in the town."

Samuel brushed away a tear. When they reached Lipoppo, the two men stood awkwardly facing each other.

"I want you to have this, Samuel."

Father Albert handed Harbinger a package wrapped in faded Christmas paper.

"What is it?"

"Go ahead, see what it is."

Samuel opened the wrapping paper. It was Father Albert's Latin dictionary. A note written on the title page read, "Just in case you forget that *ubi* means 'where' and *ibi* means 'there.'" Harbinger could not hold back his tears.

"Albert, come with me into church. Somehow I feel God will not let you leave his service quite so easily. Leave me your address in London."

"It is in the Latin dictionary..

The two priests knelt and said the rosary. When they had finished, Albert stood up and left the church.

* * * * * *

Father Albert's elopement left Bishop Harbinger in charge of two parishes. Twice a week Obani would drive Harbinger to Woomba - on Fridays to hear confessions, and on Sundays to say Mass. The increased commuting was burdensome, but not nearly as troublesome as the conduct of some of Harbinger's friends and parishioners.

On the theory that any single woman in Lipoppo might have designs on their bishop, Zamba and several other devout church members adopted what would have to be called a form

186

of vigilantism. Zamba, for example, would sit in church during confessions and keep track of the time an unmarried woman spent in the confessional. If he thought the woman was spending too much time reciting her sins, he would stand outside the door of the confessional and start to clear his throat. If the confession continued, Zamba would start to cough loudly. And if this still didn't work, he would knock on the confessional door.

Hestern, the carpenter, was even bolder in his methods. He would stop single women in the street and remind them of the hellfire that awaited any woman who slept with a priest, let alone a bishop. Harbinger was even worried that his close friend Mobeki might join the ranks of the vigilantes. Trying to appear matter-of-fact, Mobeki had asked the bishop to explain what the church meant by a "near occasion of sin."

* * * * * *

Two faxes from Boston reached Bishop Samuel several weeks after his return to Lipoppo. The first was from an elated Mark. On Patriot's Day in April, he ran in the Boston Marathon and had finished eleventh. The second fax was from Martha. She wrote that she and Mark had created a company and had begun selling nativity sets to Harvard faculty. They had already sold fifty-eight personalized magi sets and had orders for eighteen more. Martha also noted that several recent purchasers wanted their pets included in the scene. They had agreed to a Saint Bernard dog and a rabbit but said no to a snake and a hamster. Martha's fax did not ask after her own cheetah cub that she had left with her father in Lipoppo.

As May 15 began to loom on the horizon, Samuel Harbinger prepared to leave for Harvard and the honorary degree presentation.

* * * * * *

Mark paced up and down waiting for the airport gate to open.

Martha sat in a chair and nervously played with her hair. They were waiting for Bishop Harbinger to disembark from the plane. A terrorist scare at London's Heathrow Airport had delayed the take-off of the London–Boston flight for more than twelve hours. Bishop Harbinger was to be awarded his honorary degree in two hours. With luck, thought Mark, the bishop could still make it to the special convocation. A movable gate was wheeled into place and Harbinger was the first passenger off the plane.

Mark took the bishop's carry-on luggage. "Do you have anything else, sir?"

"Just my bike, Mark."

"Can we come back for it later?"

"No. It will be at the luggage carousel. The flight attendant called ahead to make sure it was taken off first."

Martha had kept silent for as long as she could.

"As of yesterday, Bishop, the number of nativity sets we have sold has increased to ninety-three. We are beginning to get orders from New York. We have been told to search for a group of investors. Do you know what a group of investors would look like, Bishop Samuel?"

* * * * * *

A taxicab sat idling outside the airport terminal. A police car sat behind the cab.

Mark shouted to the taxi driver. "Let's go. Harvard Yard as soon as possible."

Harbinger rummaged through his pockets. "Mark, I can't find my instructions about what color hood and robe to wear. I remember the robe should be crimson, but I forget the color of the hood."

Martha interjected. "Bishop Samuel, a green one would look nice."

"You can't choose a color because you like it, Martha. There are strict rules for these things. President Wedgwood told me the rules go back to the late Middle Ages."

Mark laughed. "We never had an early or a late Middle Ages in Kenya, Bishop. So how can you be expected to know the right color for a graduation hood?"

When the cab reached the Harvard campus, Bishop Harbinger jumped out and hurried through crowds of alumni who had come to witness the conferral of Harbinger's honorary degree. A man from Miami, Florida, recognized him.

"Bishop Harbinger, Roland Sekkoes is my name. Could I take your picture with my son? He just lost his girlfriend in a boating accident. It would mean a lot to him."

"Of course."

When the picture taking was over, the father handed Harbinger an envelope.

"I was going to give you this after the convocation. Thank you for all you have done for Palestine."

Harbinger pushed the envelope into his pants' pocket.

"Thank you. I must go or I'll be late for the program. I will read your letter after the ceremony."

"Don't forget to open it."

"I won't."

When Bishop Harbinger finally reached the robing room, he saw that there were only a few robes and hoods left. He picked up a crimson robe but its zipper was broken. A second crimson robe had a large tear on the right shoulder. Unfortunately, there was no Vatican tailor ready to sew up the tear. Harbinger picked up a third crimson robe from under a chair. It didn't fit perfectly, but it fit well enough. Having secured a robe, he now went in search of a hood.

A professor sat by the door, and the bishop asked him, "Sir, I'm getting an honorary degree of Doctor of Laws at this special convocation. Do you know what color hood I'm supposed to wear?"

"Let me give you some advice from the Roman poet Horace. *Parturient montes, nascetur ridiculus mus.*"

"I'm sorry, sir. I don't know Latin that well."

"Roughly translated it means 'Who cares!' Put on whatever hood you want. In real life, I have a PhD in classical languages from Yale, but I'm going to walk in today's academic convocation as a PhD in physics from Harvard. You're welcome to join me— just put on a gold hood over your crimson robe and let's be off. You'll see academic cross-dressing is fun. You can live out your fantasies."

Samuel Harbinger rummaged through a pile of hoods.

"Is this one gold? I'm color-blind. It looks green to me but that usually means it looks gold to everyone else."

"It looks gold to me."

Harbinger threw the hood over his Harvard robe. "Okay, let's go."

"By the way, my cross-dressing friend, where are you from?"

"A village in Kenya called Lipoppo."

"Lipoppo! What a great name for a village! Do you have a university?"

"No, but we have an AIDS clinic. I am trying to build a new one."

"What do you do for a living?

"I'm a bishop—the Bishop of Lipoppo."

"*Semper Africam aliquid novi afferre.*"

"What does that mean?"

"I forgot you don't understand Latin. There was a time when all bishops did. Roughly translated it means 'Africa is full of surprises.'"

* * * * * *

President Wedgwood paced nervously as he waited to take his position at the end of the academic procession. A look of relief passed over his face when Wedgwood saw Bishop Harbinger and Francis Baellert running along the line of robed faculty..

"Samuel, I was worried that I would have to confer your honorary degree *in absentia* and give the address myself."

"The plane from London was late because of a terrorist scare, and on top of that, I showed up at the head of the procession. Luckily, I met Francis. He told me at an academic convocation like this, the featured speaker walks at the end of the procession with the president of the university."

"Yes. Dignitaries come last in academic processions. By the way, I forgot you were color-blind. You have on a gold hood for science not a purple hood for law. We'll have to make a quick substitution."

"President Wedgwood, is it so important that I wear the right color hood as long as I receive the right degree?"

"In academia, the color of robes and hoods are emblems of your rank and status. In your profession, Samuel, the color of clothing is also a sign of status. In Catholicism, don't priests and monks wear black or brown robes; bishops like you, purple; and cardinals, red, and the pope white."

"Yes, but—"

"Samuel, the convocation is about to start. Everyone is looking forward to your remarks. Just watch out for the norms of political correctness."

"What do you mean?"

"Just say 'she' when you'd say 'he' and 'her' when you'd say 'his.'"

"That's all there is to it?"

"Basically, yes."

"Should I also say 'woman' for 'man'?"

"It can't hurt, Samuel."

* * * * * *

John Wedgwood walked to the podium and looked out over

the dizzying array of colored gowns and hoods of the Harvard faculty.

"Members of the Harvard community and distinguished guests. I am here today to introduce the recipient of Harvard's Honorary Doctor of Laws Degree. Usually no one ever remembers what a speaker says at a university commencement, let alone a special convocation, but today might just be an exception. Samuel Harbinger is a man of great wisdom and humility—a man who has been awarded the Nobel Peace Prize, a man who has addressed the General Assembly of the United Nations, and a man about to be awarded an honorary degree from this great university. I have asked Bishop Harbinger to tell us one of those magical stories of his village of Lipoppo in Kenya. Those who are assigned the role of introducer must realize that it is the introduced that has been selected to speak. So I give you my friend Bishop Samuel Harbinger, who will transport us into a kingdom ruled by wise elephants and stubborn giraffes."

"Thank you, President Wedgwood. I am flattered by your introduction. I am also aware of the great honor your university has bestowed on me by awarding this degree at a special convocation."

A wooden box had been placed at the podium so Harbinger could be seen over the microphones. Just as he laid a copy of his remarks on the podium, however, a gust of wind blew the pages away.

Harbinger shrugged humorously. "I was planning to speak to you this afternoon about my housekeeper Bagua and her ostrich egg. I guess God prefers that I speak on a different topic. God speaks to us in different ways. She may speak to us through a rain shower, or as we have just seen, she may speak to us through a gust of wind. She has her plans for us—we must always realize that her plans, whether they are for you or for me, or for womankind as a whole, are based on her love for us. The Shebrew prophets understood this when they said ..."

President Wedgwood virtually somersaulted his way up to the

podium. He whispered in Harbinger's ear. "Samuel, forget what I said about 'him' and 'her' and political correctness. Speak the way you always do."

"Are you absolutely sure? I was about to refer to the Holy Trinity as Mother, Son, and Holy Spirit."

John Wedgwood winced. "Yes, I'm absolutely sure."

Harbinger turned back to his audience.

"Given God's preferences, today I will talk to you about Serena and her zebra. From the day Serena was born, she never spoke. Her mother did not know what to do. The doctor in Nairobi said that Serena would get better as she got older. The local shaman prescribed a mixture of herbs and roots, but still Serena did not speak. People in the village began to say that an evil spirit possessed her.

"One day Serena's mother came upon a zebra calf sitting in the tall grass. The calf was bleating, calling out for his family. Serena's mother could see that one of his legs was broken. She took the calf home and put a splint on the animal's leg. The next morning, Serena's mother was amazed to see Serena petting the baby animal and the animal licking Serena's cheeks in return.

"Day after day, Serena and the baby zebra played with each other. When his leg healed, the zebra allowed Serena to ride on his back, and in turn, Serena taught the zebra how to kick a soccer ball.

"One day Serena's mother went to visit her sister who lived five kilometers from Lipoppo along the Woomba road. Serena and the baby zebra tagged along behind her. Suddenly, they came upon a small herd of zebras on their way to the water hole. The zebra calf looked at Serena and licked her cheek. Serena took off a medal that her mother had given her and put it over the animal's neck. The calf made a low, almost pathetic sound.

"'Don't cry. You belong with them. This medal will keep you safe.'

"Serena's mother looked at her daughter in disbelief. Her child had just spoken.

"The zebra began to follow the herd but then stopped and came back. He shook his head and kicked dirt in the air as if the animal were angry. Serena looked at her friend and then gave him a big hug.

"'Okay. I promise. I will speak.'

"And Serena did from that day forward.

"Every now and again, Serena's zebra would return to Lipoppo for a visit. Once the zebra even brought his daughter.

"Such, my friends and benefactors of this great university, is the power of love. Truly it does conquer all."

* * * * * *

After his speech and the award of the honorary degree, Bishop Harbinger accompanied John Wedgwood to the president's house for dinner with the Board of Overseers. When he took off his academic gown, Harbinger felt something in his pants' pocket. He remembered the letter from the man who had stopped him for a picture. When he opened the envelope, he saw a three million dollar check signed by a Roland Polycarp Sekkoes and made payable to Harvard University. In the lower left-hand corner, there was a notation that the money should be spent "as Bishop Harbinger directs."

Flushed with excitement, Harbinger asked President Wedgwood to join him on the patio for a brief conversation.

"John, look at this check. Mr. Sekkoes handed it to me today in the Harvard Yard. He thanked me for helping Palestine. With these three million dollars, I can finish building Lipoppo's AIDS clinic."

"Before you spend the money, Samuel, let me call one of our alumni in Miami. I want to know more about this Mr. Sekkoes - where did he go to school, what does he do for a living, who are his bankers?"

Five minutes later, a somber-looking president of Harvard University joined his guests in the dining room.

"Samuel, I'm afraid you're going to have to look someplace else for your three million dollars."

"Why?"

"According to my sources, Roland Polycarp Sekkoes is heavily involved in drug trafficking in south Florida. My sources also tell me that Sekkoes is about to be indicted for money laundering.. Accepting money from known money launderers like Sekkoes would embarrass the university."

"But think of all the good Harvard could do with the money. Isn't it better to take it? Accepting the money does not condone how it was acquired or where it came from."

"If Judas offered you the thirty pieces of silver he earned for betraying Jesus, it sounds like you would take it."

Harbinger paused. "Taking the money does not contribute to Jesus' suffering, and spending it relieves the suffering of others. So, yes, I guess I would take it."

Chapter Eleven
The Death of God's Servant

After dinner with the Board of Overseers, President Wedgwood escorted Bishop Harbinger to Harvard's Memorial Hall for an alumni reception in his honor. As they entered the building Francis Baellert pulled the bishop aside.

"Samuel, I think you'd better excuse yourself from the reception."

"Why, Francis?"

"The Associated Press is reporting that Pope Linus has suffered a seizure and has been hospitalized. The Vatican has scheduled a press conference, which will air in ten minutes. Isn't the Vatican pretty tight-lipped about the pope's health?"

"Yes, the joke is that the Vatican will admit the pope's sick only after he's dead. If they have called a press conference, Pope Linus must be seriously ill. Francis, is there a television set somewhere nearby so I can find out what has happened?"

"Come to my office. It's a three-minute walk from here."

* * * * *

A grim-faced Cardinal Sebastiano Bagonninni, Vatican secretary of state, faced a room filled with reporters. Behind him stood Cardinal Martin Jensen, prefect of the Congregation for Bishops.

"At approximately 2:30 this morning, Pope Linus suffered a massive stroke and was taken to Gemelli Hospital. Doctor Marcello Tussi, chief of neurology at the hospital, has informed me that the Holy Father is in critical condition. Complicating treatment is a bullet lodged in the pope's chest from an attempted assassination almost two decades ago. Immediately after this press conference, Doctor Tussi will provide a detailed report on the pope's medical condition. I'll take questions now."

The cardinal nervously fingered his jeweled pectoral cross as he struggled to hold back his emotions.

A reporter from Milan's *Corriere della Sera* asked the first question. "Who found the pope?"

"Sister Consuela, the pope's housekeeper. She heard Fides barking. She went into the pope's bedroom and found His Holiness on the floor."

"Is the pope alert, Your Eminence?" The reporter from *Corriere della Sera* asked a follow-up question.

"No. At the moment, the Holy Father has lost consciousness. Questions about Pope Linus' medical condition should be saved for Doctor Tussi."

"What procedures are being put in place to administer the church during this time?" The reporter from Turin's *La Stampa* took up the questioning.

Cardinal Bagonninni chose his words carefully. "As most of you know, the camerlengo, or chamberlain of the Catholic Church, administers the day-to-day operations of the Holy See if and when a pope dies. Pope Linus appointed Cardinal Josef Vortel to that position several years ago. At the moment, Cardinal Vortel has been on a two-day visit to Assisi. I spoke to the camerlengo myself and informed him of the pope's condition. He is returning to Rome as soon as possible."

"Your Eminence." A reporter from the *Los Angeles Times* asked the next question. "Let us suppose the pope remains in a coma for weeks or months. Are there procedures in place for removing him from office?"

"I will defer a discussion of these matters until the camerlengo arrives back in the Vatican. In the meantime, I ask you all to pray for His Holiness' recovery. Now, gentlemen, if you will excuse me, I have many matters to attend to. Doctor Tussi will answer your medical questions."

The reporter from the *Los Angelus Times* scribbled on a notepad. "Bagonninni is caught with his scarlet pants down. He knows there are no rules covering a pope's removal, but he's not going to admit it publicly."

* * * * * *

When Cardinal Bagonninni announced the pope's stroke, Bishop Harbinger knelt on the floor of Francis Baellert's office, and crossing himself, prayed silently for his friend.

"I must fly to Rome as soon as possible, Francis. Maybe I can help Pope Linus in some small way."

Baellert turned off the television set. "Samuel, I have to stay at the reception. I'll have a university driver pick you up and take you to Logan Airport whenever you're ready."

* * * * * *

Monsignor Paolo Remigi, Pope Linus' private secretary, knew that the pontiff did not have much time to live. Although the doctors had initially been able to stabilize the pope's vital signs, his condition had grown progressively worse during the last hour. Remigi had hoped that Cardinal Vortel, the camerlengo, would have arrived back in Rome in time to administer the last rites to the pope. Unfortunately, due to heavy rains, Cardinal Vortel's flight from Assisi was delayed. A helicopter sent by the prime minister to fetch the cardinal also had to turn back because of the weather. Remigi knew he would have to be the one to give the last rites to Pope Linus.

When the room was cleared of all but necessary medical staff, Remigi took a small bottle of consecrated oil out of his pocket. Reciting the *Pater Noster*, Remigi poured some oil on his fingertips and slowly traced the sign of the cross over the pope's eyes, ears, nostrils, lips, hands, and feet. After he had finished the anointing, Remigi noticed that the pope seemed to be trying to point his finger at a table near the hospital room door. The only things on the table were a hospital notepad and a pencil. Puzzled, Remigi picked up the pad and pencil and laid them on the bed next to the pontiff. Pope Linus lifted up the pencil and laboriously drew the letter E on the top page of the notepad.

"Holy Father, I do not understand."

Pope Linus lifted up the pencil again, and this time he drew an N and then a V.

Suddenly Remigi understood. "Holy Father, you are spelling out a word, aren't you?"

Pope Linus nodded imperceptibly.

"Is the word 'envelope'?"

The pope picked up the pencil and drew a Y on a piece of notepaper.

"You want to tell me something about an envelope?"

Remigi wrote out the alphabet in large, capital letters on the notepaper. "Point to the letters, Holy Father. It will be easier for you."

The pope pointed to the letters D and E.

"What comes next, Holy Father?"

Pope Linus pointed to the letter S and then to the letter K.

Remigi looked jubilant. "The word is DESK, isn't it? You're telling me about an envelope in a desk. Where is the desk?"

The pope pointed to the letters that spelled the word STUDY.

"So Holiness, there is an envelope in the desk of your study. Do you want me to open the envelope and read the contents?"

Pope Linus pointed to the letter Y.

"And what should I do with the letter after I read it?"

This time, Pope Linus pointed to the letters TOBAG.

Suddenly the pontiff's body became rigid, and he fell back into his bed. Remigi rang for Doctor Tussi. When the doctor looked at the pope's monitor, Tussi pulled Remigi aside.

"Monsignor, you'll have to leave the room. Pope Linus is suffering another seizure. If there are any last minute matters that require attention, see to them now."

* * * * * *

Remigi left Gemelli Hospital and took a taxi to the Vatican. He felt a sense of urgency about the envelope in the pope's study. The Swiss Guards on duty outside the pope's quarters snapped to attention when Remigi unlocked the door to the papal apartment. He hurried inside and sat at Pope Linus' desk. When he opened the top drawer, he saw a box full of assorted pills the pope had managed to avoid taking despite the vigilance of Sister Consuela.

Next to the pills was a sealed envelope on top of a pile of correspondence. Remigi broke the seal and read the Latin document inside. It was an *in pectore* appointment of Bishop Harbinger to the College of Cardinals. By its terms, the appointment was to take effect on Harbinger's forty-fifth birthday or at such earlier date as the pope determined. But Remigi could not understand the last piece of the puzzle—the letters TOBAG.

Then, as if hit by a thunderbolt, Remigi realized what the pope was trying to communicate. TOBAG meant TO BAGONNINNI. Unless a secret or *in pectore* appointment to the Sacred College was proclaimed publicly before a nominating pope's death, the appointment became invalid. The pope wanted Harbinger's appointment given to Cardinal Bagonninni, so the secretary of state could publicly announce it.

Remigi grabbed the letter and hurried along the corridor to Cardinal Bagonninni's office.

As he entered the outer office, Remigi headed straight for the door to the cardinal's private study.

"And where do you think you are going, Monsignor Remigi?" Bagonninni's assistant blocked the doorway to the study. Those who had to deal with the cardinal's assistant found him arrogant and rude. No one could understand why the good-natured Bagonninni kept him as his assistant. The most prevalent explanation was that the assistant provided Bagonninni with one-stop shopping when it came to Vatican gossip. The assistant had his ear everywhere

"I must see Cardinal Bagonninni about this letter. It is urgent."

"Let me see the letter, Remigi."

"No, it is for the secretary of states' eyes only."

"Nothing gets on his desk unless I see it first."

Remigi slammed his fist on the assistant's desk. "If you don't let me into Bagonninni's study, I'll break down the door myself."

"Go right ahead, Monsignor. The cardinal is not here at the moment."

"Where is he?"

"He is on his way to the airport to meet the camerlengo."

"Get him on his cell phone."

Just then, the bells of the *Arco delle Campane* began to toll. Seconds later, bells all over Rome took up the mournful cadence. Pope Linus II was dead. Harbinger's *in pectore* appointment to the College of Cardinals was invalid.

"Forget the phone call." Remigi pushed Bagonninni's assistant out of the way and left the cardinal's office.

* * * * * *

A slightly stooped man in his early seventies, the camerlengo, Cardinal Josef Vortel, performed the ancient death rituals for a pope. Taking a silver mallet, he tapped the pope's forehead and called out Benat, his Christian name. When the pope did not respond after the third tap, Cardinal Vortel intoned the words. "*Papa mortuus est.* The pope is truly dead."

Then with key Vatican officials and senior members of the College of Cardinals looking on, the camerlengo removed the fisherman's ring from the fourth finger of Pope Linus' right hand. Taking a hammer, Vortel struck the ring several times until it broke into pieces. The camerlengo then took the pope's lead seal and broke it as well. Everyone in the room understood the significance of what was taking place. Pope Linus' ring and seal were symbols of his authority. With both of them broken, his pontificate ended. The day-by-day government of the church now devolved on the camerlengo and the College of Cardinals.

One act remained. As the dignitaries stood by, Vortel formally locked the door to Pope Linus' living quarters. Then making an X out of red ribbons, he affixed it to the front door. The X would remain on the door until a new pope was elected.

As the others filed past the entrance to the pope's quarters, Cardinal Bagonninni put his arm on Cardinal Jensen's shoulder.

"You are the clear favorite to succeed Pope Linus, Martin. But you know the adage: he that enters the conclave pope comes out cardinal."

"There are exceptions. Cardinal Ratzinger went into the conclave the clear frontrunner and came out Benedict XVI."

* * * * * *

Later that night, the camerlengo telephoned Paolo Remigi, Pope Linus' personal secretary.

"Paolo, could you come to my apartment later tonight, say at nine-thirty? I have a question to ask you. It is a matter of some importance."

"Of course, Cardinal Vortel."

"Good. I will send my car to pick you up."

* * * * * *

The camerlengo greeted Remigi warmly at the door to his apartment.

"Thank you for coming on such short notice, Paolo. It was a sad day today. My heart broke when I had to remove Pope Linus' ring."

"Mine, too. But you said you had a question to ask me—an important question?"

"Yes, but first a glass of wine. A Riesling perhaps?"

"That would be fine."

The cardinal poured two glasses of wine and motioned Remigi to join him at a table and two easy chairs at the far end of his living room. After putting the glasses of wine on the table, Vortel walked over to a mahogany sideboard to choose some music.

"Paolo, do you like Wagner?"

"Yes, but only in small doses."

Vortel smiled. "That's a polite way of saying 'no.' Let me put on Verdi's *Requiem* instead."

"Thank you, Eminence. For me, Wagner is long no matter how short the excerpt. But the question you wished to ask me, what is it?"

"I understand you found a letter from Pope Linus."

"Yes, it was a failed attempt to elevate Bishop Harbinger to a cardinal."

"I received a second letter from the Holy Father. He instructed me to open it only after his death. Did the pope ever mention sending me such a letter?"

"No."

"You were the Pope's secretary. If he had sent such a letter, would you have known about it."

"Yes, I believe so."

"What if the letter were written in the pope's own hand?"

"Then I might not have known about it. The pope did write some personal correspondence in his own hand but he rarely did so."

"Can you recognize Pope Linus' handwriting?"

"Of course, Cardinal Vortel."

The camerlengo handed Remigi a letter.

"Is this the pontiff's handwriting and signature?"

Remigi looked carefully at the letter. "Yes, it is, Cardinal Vortel."

"Are you sure, Paolo? Look again."

"Yes, it is his handwriting and signature. I'm sure of it."

"Thank you, Monsignor. Would you have another glass of Riesling?"

"Yes and some more of the *Requiem*."

* * * * * *

The phone rang just after Samuel Harbinger had finished packing for his trip to Rome. Tired and saddened by Pope Linus' death, he debated whether to take the call. Something, however, told him he should.

"Samuel, is that you?"

Harbinger recognized the voice of Paolo Remigi.

"Monsignor Remigi, Pope Linus' death must have been a terrible tragedy for you. He loved you like a son."

"Yes, I think of him every waking hour. But I am calling not about his death but about another matter—one that involves you."

"Me?"

"Yes. Pope Linus left an envelope in his desk drawer. It appointed you a member of the College of Cardinals but postponed announcing the appointment until your forty-fifth birthday or some earlier date as the pope saw fit. Unfortunately, the appointment was never proclaimed before Pope Linus died."

"So it lapsed?"

"Unfortunately, yes. Leaving a letter in the drawer is not the way to appoint someone to office. Still, I wanted you to know that despite his not making you a cardinal, Pope Linus had enormous respect and admiration for you. He told me once that with your fresh energy and new ideas, you were the best thing that has happened to the Catholic Church since Francis of Assisi. Do you know why the Holy Father delayed making the announcement?"

Harbinger thought a moment. "No. The only thing I can recall was something he said to me during his trip to Lipoppo. As he was dressing for Mass, he put his hand on my shoulder and looked me in the eyes. 'Hurry up and grow older, Samuel. With some gray hairs, it will be easier to introduce your brand of Christianity to Catholics throughout the world.' Perhaps the pope thought I was too young to be appointed a cardinal. Whatever the reason, it was God's will that I not participate in the conclave to find Pope Linus' successor."

"Or maybe God wants you to participate in a different way. When will you come to Rome?"

"I will be there tomorrow, Paolo."

* * * * * *

Father Cropsy met Bishop Harbinger at Leonardo da Vinci Airport.

"You're in time for Pope Linus' funeral Mass and burial, but just remember one thing; Rome is not the same city as it was even a week ago. Since Pope Linus died, it's all politics. Every member of the College of Cardinals is being put under a microscope. Cardinal X is not fluent in English. Cardinal Y is rumored to have cancer. Cardinal Z likes handsome seminarians. Some of the rumors border on the fanciful—that on his deathbed, Pope Linus had a vision of the future. He supposedly cried out 'cataclysm dot org backslash.' Bloggers are going wild with speculation. Then there's the rumor that Michelangelo's statue of Moses in the

Church of San Pietro in Vincoli spoke, in German mind you, and said the next pope would be from Glasgow. The press calls this one The Glaswegian Prophecy."

"Rumors and speculation are the work of the devil, Ignatius. The Holy Spirit will guide the cardinals to the right person to govern the church. If that person happens to be Glaswegian, so be it." Harbinger was proud of himself. He finally understood what the word Glaswegian meant without having to ask.

Cropsy lifted Harbinger's suitcase and bicycle off the baggage carousel.

"There's been talk about you, Samuel. The thought of electing a Nobel laureate as pope intrigues some of the German cardinals."

"Ignatius, the church is not ready for an African pope even if he won the Nobel Peace Prize. And if I'm wrong about that, I wouldn't be the one chosen."

"Why not?"

"I'm too small for the Holy Spirit to see."

"But you have your miter. It makes you taller."

"But still not tall enough, Ignatius. Can we take a bicycle ride to the Piazza Navona, or will it be too crowded with would-be popes?"

"Of course, we can go, but rest assured our bike ride will be mentioned in tomorrow's tabloids and rumor mills."

* * * * * *

Ignatius Cropsy and Samuel Harbinger watched live footage of cardinals entering the conclave area on a television screen.

Who goes in first," asked Harbinger?

"You must have learned in the seminary that there are three ranks of cardinals - cardinal bishops, cardinal priests, and cardinal deacons. Cardinal bishops lead the procession into the conclave area, followed by cardinal priests and finally by cardinal deacons."

"It's amazing to think of what's going on, Ignatius. The Sistine

Chapel is about to become the world's most watched voting booth. Michelangelo must be pleased."

Harbinger pointed to the TV monitor.

"There goes Jensen in."

"He's the odds-on favorite. Our esteemed prefect of the Congregation for Bishops has been campaigning for the job for a long time. He has widespread support from conservatives—especially those from Latin America and Eastern Europe."

Harbinger nodded his head. "And he looks like a pope, doesn't he?"

Cropsy opened a Coca-Cola. "Yes. The Americans would say he's from central casting—that has to influence some of his colleagues."

"Central casting? What does that mean, Ignatius?"

"It means that he fits the model of an ideal pope—he's smart, friendly, and photogenic, dignified in appearance, speaks seven languages, and has that intangible something called star quality."

"Can other people be from central casting or is it only for popes?"

"Anyone can be from central casting."

"What about Obani, the postman in Lipoppo? He just looks like a postman should look like."

"Then he's from central casting."

"I will tell Obani that. It will make him happy."

This time Cropsy pointed to the television screen. "There goes Plimpton—the darling of the left. He might get the job if Jensen and his conservative supporters don't have the votes. But you always have to remember one thing about Plimpton. He's an American. Some cardinals still worry about choosing a pope from a superpower."

"Plimpton looks like he's from central casting, too."

Cropsy slowly sipped his Coca-Cola. "He does, doesn't he? The Holy Spirit may have to choose between Gregory Peck and Cary Grant."

"Who are they?"

"Screen idols."

"But what will happen if neither Jensen nor Plimpton can get the necessary two-thirds vote to win?"

"That's when the dark horse appears."

"Who would that dark horse be?"

"It may be you, Samuel."

"Stop saying that, Ignatius. I'm not a cardinal."

"Haven't you ever studied canon law?"

"I did, but it was not my best subject in the seminary."

"Well, canon law is clear. You don't have to be a cardinal to be elected pope. In fact, you don't have to be a bishop, priest, or deacon. If a layperson were ever elected, he'd have to be ordained a priest and a bishop before becoming pope."

"So Obani could be elected pope?"

"Theoretically, yes."

Harbinger paused a moment lost in thought. "Signor Chimati, the proprietor of *Dignitas*, called me today."

"Chimati called you?"

"Yes."

"What did he say? Chimati doesn't call clients very often."

"He told me that I was *papabile* and should get business cards with a picture of Jesus on them."

"Chimati called you *papabile*?"

"Yes. What does the word mean, Ignatius?"

"It means you've got what it takes to be pope."

* * * * * *

Bishop Vergilio Patti, the papal master of ceremonies, stood outside the Sistine Chapel. Beside him were two senior Vatican officials, the commandant of the Swiss Guards and the prefect of the papal household.

"Commandant, what's your count?"

"I counted one hundred twenty cardinals go into the conclave."

"And prefect, what's your number?"

"The same—one hundred twenty."

Patti scanned his master list of cardinal electors. "Good. One hundred twenty is the right number. There are twenty-five more cardinals, but they are not eligible to vote because they're over eighty years of age."

Suddenly, a technician came running out of the Sistine Chapel. He hurried over to the master of ceremonies.

"We've swept the conclave area, Bishop Patti. It's free of bugs, dogs, and electronic devices but …"

"But what?"

"Could I speak with you privately, Bishop Patti?"

"Yes, of course." The master of ceremonies excused himself and walked down a corridor with the technician.

"Your Excellency, there are actually one hundred twenty-one cardinals in there, not one hundred twenty."

"How can that be? We counted one hundred twenty go in."

"Well, one was already in the conclave area before the others proceeded in."

"How could that be?"

"One of the overage cardinals hid under the bed."

"Who was that?"

"Cardinal Tung Bin Kim from Korea. Kim turned eighty the day before Pope Linus died. According to the rules, cardinals who celebrate their eightieth birthdays *before* the day when the Apostolic See becomes vacant are ineligible to participate in the election of a new pope."

"So Kim can't participate."

"Well, Kim says that since he celebrates his eightieth birthday in Korea a day later than in Rome, he should be treated as turning eighty not on the day before the Apostolic See became vacant but on the day the Apostolic See became vacant. According to his logic, he can participate in the conclave. The camerlengo, however, does not agree with his reading of the rule. Kim's peeved and said he won't leave his room in the Domus. He fully intends to participate in the conclave no matter what the camerlengo does or says. Hence the one hundred twenty-one number."

"Kim can't just bully his way into the conclave. Tell His Eminence that if he doesn't vacate his room immediately I'll have him dragged out by the Swiss Guards. Anything else?"

"Just one thing more, Bishop Patti. One of the electors won't give up his mobile phone. He says he is being treated for depression and needs to be able to contact his therapist at a moment's notice."

"It is Cardinal Somple, isn't it?"

"Yes."

"I've spoken to Somple about this already. He's a cranky old man who is used to getting his way. He's convinced that if he nags long enough, I'll give up and let him bring his phone into the conclave. Well, that's not going to happen. There is a phone installed in my room at the Domus. It's for situations like this. Tell him he can use it if necessary."

The master of ceremonies walked back to the commandant of the guards and the prefect of the papal household.

"Is there a problem, Patti?" The commandant looked concerned.

"Not anymore. The clampdown is complete. Do either of you have anything further?"

Both men shook their heads.

"Then it's time to get the process moving. This could be a long conclave."

Bishop Patti cleared his throat and boomed out the centuries-old words that open a papal election.

"*Extra Omnes*! Everyone not permitted in the conclave area must leave."

The commandant and prefect shook hands with Patti.

"Our paths must part, my friends. I must go into the conclave."

A few minutes later, Patti locked the door to the Apostolic Palace from the inside. For a minute, the key would not turn in the lock—it was as if the Sistine Chapel were still not ready to begin the balloting. Finally, with a scraping sound, the key turned in the lock. Patti breathed a sigh of relief and put the key in his pocket. When he would take it out was anybody's guess.

* * * * * *

The cardinal electors would not leave the sealed-off area until they had elected a pope. To that end, the electors would cast ballots four times a day, two ballots in the morning session of the conclave and two ballots in the afternoon session. To be selected, a candidate must obtain the support of two-thirds of the one hundred twenty electors voting. A quick calculation showed that a candidate would need eighty votes to win. After each session, the used ballots and any notes pertaining to these ballots are burned in a metal stove that stands just outside the Sistine Chapel. Black smoke rises if no one has received the necessary votes, white smoke if someone is selected.

Chapter Twelve
Habemus Papam

After two days of inconclusive balloting, Bishop Harbinger was quoted in the local press as asking Catholics to gather in the piazzas of Rome to pray to the Holy Spirit to bring a quick end to the conclave. In response to his request, large crowds filled the numerous piazzas of the city. The largest crowd—perhaps as many as seventy-five thousand people—jammed into St. Peter's Square. Rosary beads in hand, Bishop Harbinger biked to the many piazzas where the crowds had gathered.

* * * * * *

On the evening after the second full day of balloting, the camerlengo hosted an informal dinner in the Borgia Apartments. As espresso was served, the Archbishop of New York, Cardinal Richard Plimpton, rose to speak to the cardinal electors. Gone was the cardinal's business-like manner that was his hallmark.

"Black smoke has risen over St. Peter's Square four times in the last two days. As the balloting has proceeded, neither Cardinal

Jensen nor I have been able to attract the necessary eighty votes for election. Cardinal Jensen comes closest with sixty-one votes on the first ballot. I had forty-five votes on that same ballot. The tally in the last vote today shows how much our initial support has eroded. Cardinal Jensen received forty-four votes and I received thirty-one. In my view, neither Cardinal Jensen nor I can win."

Plimpton stared at his rival. "Given the deadlock, I suggest Cardinal Jensen and I both withdraw and allow the conclave to search for a new candidate."

A disgruntled Jensen stood up and pointed his finger at the archbishop of New York. "If my esteemed colleague wishes to withdraw from the voting, then by all means let him do so. I will not withdraw, however."

Plimpton threw up his hands in exasperation. "Then, Jensen, back to the voting tomorrow morning and more black smoke over St. Peter's Square."

A ninth ballot was taken the next morning and again support for Jensen and Plimpton continued to erode. The results of the tally showed thirty-eight votes for Jensen and twenty-seven for Plimpton.

As the electors prepared to go to a tenth ballot, the camerlengo rose from his seat and walked up to the altar.

"I realize that during a conclave, the Sistine Chapel is reserved for voting, prayer, and meditation. On rare occasions, however, an elector has broken this rule. I ask my colleagues to be allowed to speak now."

Cardinal Ugo Carpaccio, the dean of the College of Cardinals, struggled to his feet. "Why didn't you speak last night at dinner, Vortel?" There was a tone of reprimand in Carpaccio's voice. "You had the opportunity then."

"I couldn't."

"What do you mean 'you couldn't'? Don't be mysterious, my lord camerlengo."

"A month before he died, Pope Linus addressed a letter to

me to be read at the next conclave between the ninth and tenth ballots. That time has now come."

Jensen jumped to his feet, his face flushed with anger. "This is highly irregular, Vortel. In 1996, Pope John Paul II set out new rules governing papal elections. You know that as well as I. The pope explicitly wrote that documents left by a deceased pope for the College of Cardinals be read before the conclave begins, not after it begins."

"That is right, Cardinal Jensen. But a document addressed by the pope to one cardinal is not covered by the prohibition even though the letter is read to all the electors."

"This is a technicality, Vortel. The letter should not be read."

Cardinal Carpaccio, perhaps the most respected member of the College of Cardinals, shook his head. "Let the letter be read, Martin. Pope Linus was a good man and a good pope. We should listen to his wisdom. Go ahead, Vortel, and read the letter."

Jensen continued to object. "But this letter could be a complete fabrication—has the pope's handwriting been verified?"

Vortel glared at Jensen. "Monsignor Remigi has verified Pope Linus' handwriting. Who better than the pope's own secretary to do such a thing?" Cardinal Jensen slumped back in his chair.

Vortel took an envelope out of his attaché case.

"My Lord Camerlengo, if the cardinal electors have not selected my successor by the end of the ninth ballot, it bespeaks a deep division among them. The issues facing the church in the years ahead do not admit to easy solutions. Seminaries are empty, clergy are involved in scandal, medievalism still permeates the moral teachings of the church, and the laity deserts the sacraments. The church must respond to the needs of the historical moment. But to do so, we need a new direction—a direction that emphasizes love over rancor, forgiveness over enmity, and simplicity over pettiness. We also need a new leader to take us down new paths. I believe there is someone who can set the church on this new course. His name is Samuel Harbinger, bishop of the village of

Lipoppo in Kenya. I believe firmly that as his name attests, he is a harbinger of what awaits the church in the future.

"Therefore I ask you, Cardinal Vortel, to address the conclave on my behalf and propose Bishop Harbinger as our next pope. I know he may not be a cardinal, but why should that matter? I know that he is young, but he is wise beyond his years. I know he does not speak many languages, but he speaks the most important language—the language of the heart. He loves his God, his church, and the marginalized—the AIDS victim, the hungry, the poor, the homelrss, the disenfranchised and the forlorn and the depressed. Listen for the Holy Spirit and follow his counsel. I think he will lead you to Bishop Harbinger.

"The letter is signed, Pope Linus II, Servant of the Servants of God."

Vortel put down the letter.

Cardinal Jensen stood up to speak. "Just so I can be sure, Vortel. Tell me if the Samuel Harbinger that Pope Linus would have us elect as pope is the same Samuel Harbinger who allows animals to come to Mass, tells stories about elephants and lions, wears a dashiki instead of a cassock, rides a bicycle around Rome, and was appointed Bishop of Lipoppo by accident?"

"Yes, Jensen, it is the same person. Let me now ask you a question. Is this Jesus we worship the same Jesus who was born in a stable, rode a donkey into Jerusalem, ate with prostitutes, consorted with lepers, and drove the money-lenders out of the temple?"

On the tenth ballot, Bishop Harbinger received eighty-two votes to be pope—two more than the required two-thirds majority.

* * * * * *

Master of Ceremonies, Monsignor Patti, slipped a note under the door of the Apostolic Palace. Patti said that he would open the door from the inside to allow two electors to leave the conclave for several hours.

Patti's note stated that any mention of the trip outside the conclave was forbidden under pain of excommunication.

* * * * * *

A limousine slipped out of the back entrance of the Vatican with a driver and two passengers.

"Driver, take us to the Piazza Navona." Cardinal Sebastiano Bagonninni sat in the backseat dressed in a plain cassock. Only his gold pectoral cross and the red trim on his cassock showed his rank. Next to him in a dark business suit sat the camerlengo, Cardinal Josef Vortel.

"Sebastiano, will his friend Cropsy be there?"

Bagonninni nodded. "Yes, Josef, he has been sent for."

"Does he know the reason?"

"No, but he's no fool. I'm sure he can figure it out."

The camerlengo looked at the secretary of state with affection. "You must resign your post next month when you turn seventy-five. Will you miss the excitement of being secretary of state, Sebastiano?"

"To some extent. But I look forward more to putting my spiritual life in order. The musty air of the Curia is not a place for prayer and meditation."

"Where will you go, Sebastiano?"

"I don't know, but God will make his wishes known." Bagonninni fingered his pectoral cross unconsciously. "But he better hurry up."

Cardinal Vortel could not repress a smile. "Don't worry, Sebastiano. God will not let you slip through his fingers."

When the driver reached Piazza Navona, the two cardinals alighted from the limousine. They saw Bishop Samuel sipping an espresso at an outdoor café, his bicycle leaning on a chair. The two men walked over to his table and sat down next to him. The sudden appearance of the two cardinals startled Harbinger.

"Eminences, why did you leave the conclave? Has a pope been elected?"

The camerlengo nodded his head. "Yes."

Harbinger's eyes lit up. "Who is it?"

Cardinal Bagonninni stared at the young bishop. "The conclave elected you, Bishop Harbinger. You received a two-thirds vote on the tenth ballot—eighty-two votes out of one hundred twenty."

"You must be mistaken, Cardinal Bagonninni. Why would the Holy Spirit have chosen me?"

The secretary of state put his hand on Bishop Harbinger's shoulder. "The ways of God are mysterious, Samuel."

Just then, a breathless Ignatius Cropsy came running across the piazza weaving his way through busloads of camera-carrying tourists.

"Cropsy, they say I have been elected pope. I received eighty-two votes on the tenth ballot. Please tell them I am not equipped for the job. I had a mediocre record in the seminary and almost failed canon law. I'm hopeless with languages. I speak only English, Swahili, and a smattering of Italian. As for Latin, all I remember is that Gaul is divided into three parts. And I'm color-blind to boot."

Cropsy put his arm on his friend's shoulder. "But you are a holy man and a man whom the world trusts. As for color blindness, you have a problem seeing green. Luckily, green is an almost nonexistent color in the Vatican. Cardinals wear red, bishops and monsignors wear purple, priests and nuns wear black, and monks wear white or brown."

"And what about the people of Lipoppo? I can't leave them. I am their bishop."

Cardinal Vortel thought for a moment.

"Cardinal Bagonninni, tell me if I'm wrong. There are many episcopal models to choose from—in addition to ordinary bishops, there are suffragan bishops, titular bishops, coadjutor bishops, and auxiliary bishops. Bishop Harbinger, maybe you can be Bishop of Rome and Auxiliary Bishop of Lipoppo."

"But an auxiliary bishop of Lipoppo needs a real bishop of Lipoppo. Who would that be?"

Cardinal Bagonninni raised his hand almost jokingly. "How about me? I need a place to retire to."

Harbinger shook his head. "But you are almost seventy-five, Your Eminence. A bishop must retire at that age."

"That's not necessarily true." Father Cropsy remembered the age limitation rules. "The Holy Father can, by special dispensation, allow a bishop to continue in service to the church beyond seventy-five years of age."

Vortel chuckled. "Sebastiano, I told you God would not let you slip out of his grasp so easily."

"And what about Bagua? Without her job as housekeeper, how will she support her family?"

Father Cropsy put his hands on his hips and stood directly in front of his friend. "Enough of this nonsense, Samuel."

"Worrying about Bagua is hardly nonsense, Ignatius. She has been my housekeeper for many years."

Cropsy turned to the camerlengo.

"Your Eminence, a pope can choose his housekeeper, can't he?"

"Of course."

"Bring Bagua to Rome, Samuel. Her cooking will be much appreciated by many of us who work in the Curia."

"But she has a husband and children."

This time Cardinal Bagonninni answered. "They can come to Rome as well. I am told there are more than one hundred tasks performed in St. Peter's every day. Bagua's husband will have a pick of jobs."

"What about mmm bbbbike?" For a moment, Harbinger's childhood stutter returned. "I can't just leave it here in the mmmiddle of the Piazza Navvvona."

Cropsy had to smile. Harbinger's bicycle kept resurfacing at the oddest times and in the oddest places, he thought.

"I'll ride it back to the Vatican, Samuel. Remember, I rode it in from the airport on the day you arrived in Rome?"

"If I were mmmmade pope, could I still ride mmmmy bike around RRRRome?"

Cardinal Bagonninni appeared hesitant. "To be honest, I don't know the answer, Bishop Harbinger. The Swiss Guards may insist on having some say in this matter. But you can always ride your bike in the Vatican Gardens."

Ignatius Cropsy spoke again. "Stop casting about for excuses, Samuel. Accept the decision of the Holy Spirit."

Samuel Harbinger fell back into his chair. "God has hemmed me in on all sssides. There is no place for me to hide."

Cardinal Vortel knelt in front of Bishop Samuel. A waiter came out of the café. Curious, he walked over to Father Cropsy.

"What's going on with this clerical stuff? Are you a bunch of actors?"

"No. We're electing a pope."

"That's going on in the Vatican. Just make sure you all get out of here by lunch. Play act somewhere else. I don't want our customers thinking we cater to a bunch of weirdos." The waiter straightened some chairs and walked back into the café.

The camerlengo asked the question. "Do you accept your canonical election as Supreme Pontiff?"

Choking with emotion, Harbinger whispered, "Yes, I accept."

The new pope got up from his chair and walked over to the secretary of state. "Could I borrow your cell phone, Cardinal Bagonninni? I must make two calls."

"Of course, Your Holiness."

Samuel Harbinger looked at the secretary of state. "Am I pope already?"

"Yes, it happened when you said 'I accept.'"

Samuel dialed a number in London.

"Is that you, Albert?"

"Yes. Who is this?"

"It's Samuel. I need you to come to Rome to help me."

"Why?"

"I've been elected pope."

Samuel then dialed tre number of the post office in Lipoppo. Miraculously, Obani picked up the phone.

"This is Bishop Samuel calling. Is that you, Obani?"

"Yes."

"I want you to do me a favor."

"Of course, Bishop."

"Tell Mobeki to go visit Banda and explain that I won't be able to come home to Lipoppo for a long time. I have been elected pope. Maybe I can install a phone link so we can talk."

* * * * * *

When Bishop Harbinger walked into the Sistine Chapel, a thunderous applause greeted him.

For all to hear, the camerlengo asked Bishop Harbinger the ritual question for a second time.

"Do you accept your canonical election as Supreme Pontiff?"

"Yes. I accept."

"And by what name do you wish to be called?"

Harbinger thought a moment before responding to the camerlengo.

"Cardinal Vortel, can I keep my baptismal name?"

"Yes, many early popes did, including Saint Peter himself."

"Then I choose to be called Pope Samuel I. He led the people of Israel to a new life."

Cardinal Plimpton leaned over and whispered in Bagonninni's ear. "An African pope with a Jewish name! I think interesting times lay ahead, Your Eminence."

Bagonninni smiled at his colleague from New York. "Yes, they do. The Holy Ghost is going to give us an interesting ride."

Cardinal Vortel took the Ring of the Fisherman that a goldsmith had made for the new pope and tried to put it on the fourth finger of the new pope's right hand. Push as he might, however, the camerlengo couldn't get the ring over Samuel Harbinger's knuckle.

"We've got to get this ring on, Holiness. It is the symbol of your office."

The camerlengo looked around the Sistine Chapel. "Isn't there anyone among us who can get a ring over a knuckle?"

Cardinal Bagonninni walked toward the door of the chapel. "There must be a cook in the pantry who knows what to do. Excuse me a moment."

Ten minutes and some coconut butter later, the ring slid onto Pope Samuel's finger.

Cardinal Vortel turned to the secretary of state. "Sebastiano, now that Pope Samuel has accepted the election, I think it's time to burn the ballots cast in the ninth and tenth tallies. It will send up in white smoke and announce the election of a new pope."

* * * * * *

One by one in order of rank and seniority, the cardinal electors knelt before Pope Samuel and reverenced the Ring of the Fisherman as a sign of their loyalty and obedience.

When Cardinal Jensen came before the pope, he looked uncomfortable. "I did not vote for you, Holy Father. I offer my resignation as Prefect of the Congregation for Bishops. There is a diocese open in my native Canada. Perhaps, Your Holiness would consider me for that post."

"I accept your resignation but will not send you to Canada. I have a different post in mind for you—Vatican Secretary of State."

"What of Cardinal Bagonninni?"

"His Eminence turns seventy-five years of age next month and wishes to retire."

Tears welled in Jensen's eyes. "God has chosen his new vicar well. I have much to learn about forgiveness."

"Then you will accept the appointment?"

"Yes."

* * * * * *

Adjoining the Sistine Chapel is a small, irregularly shaped room called the Room of Tears. It is in this room that a newly elected pope is fitted for his papal vestments. No one really knows how the room got its name. One legend has it that like Jesus in the Garden of Gethsemane, it is in this room that a newly elected pope first realizes the enormity of what God requires of him. Given that realization, several popes have been known to break down and begin to cry.

When the new Pope Samuel was escorted into the room, Signor Manelli, the Vatican tailor, snapped into action. In advance of the papal conclave, Manelli had prepared three different sizes of papal soutane—a large, a medium, and a small. Whoever was elected pope should fit comfortably into one of the sizes—at least that's what Manelli assumed.

Unfortunately, his three-size strategy proved a failure. The smallest size was too big for the diminutive Pope Samuel.

Manelli blanched. "It's 1914 all over again."

The camerlengo looked at the tailor. "What do you mean, 'It's 1914 all over again,' Manelli?"

"Like Pope Samuel, Benedict XV was too small for the smallest sized soutane."

"You must work fast, Manelli. We need to introduce Pope Samuel to the crowds in ten minutes. No more."

"Cardinal Vortel, you'll have to give me more time than that. Send someone out on the balcony to stall—try a rosary in thanksgiving for the new pope's election."

"Just do what you have to do, Manelli. I'll deal with the crowds in the square."

So while the camerlengo paced up and down, impatient to introduce the new pope, the tailor worked frantically shortening sleeves, lifting hems, repositioning buttons and tucking in here and letting out there.

As the minutes went by, the camerlengo grew more and more frustrated. Finally, in exasperation bordering on desperation, he pulled a pair of scissors from Manelli's hand.

"Enough, Manelli. The crowds in the square are growing restless. They want to meet the pope and get his first blessing. I'm taking him out there."

The tailor blocked Cardinal Vortel's way. "Your Eminence, give me the scissors back. You can have me arrested, tortured, even excommunicated, but I will not let the pontiff make his first public appearance and have him trip over his soutane or have his skullcap blown off his head."

Cardinal Vortel fumed, but he handed the scissors back to Manelli.

"There are probably two hundred thousand people in the square waiting to see the new pope. You have bought five minutes more, Signor Manelli. That's all."

The tailor hurriedly sewed on the last button and affixed the pope's white cap to his head with a bobby pin borrowed from a woman on Manelli's staff. "Okay, His Holiness is ready."

By custom the senior cardinal deacon announces the name of the new pope to those in St. Peter's Square. By coincidence, Cardinal Vortel was not only camerlengo but senior most cardinal deacon as welll. Flanked by members of the three ranks of cardinals, Cardinal Vortel pushed aside the velvet tapestry and stepped out onto the central balcony of St. Peter's Basilica.

Vortel breathed a sigh of relief. The moment had come. The crowd cheered wildly. The long-awaited announcement was at hand. *"Annuntio vobis gaudium magnum.* I announce to you a great joy. *Habemus Papam.* We have a Pope." As if to squeeze every drop of suspense from the moment, Vortel adjusted the microphones and stepped back to cough.

Angry at the delay, the crowd shouted at Vortel. "His name. Tell us his name."

Cardinal Vortel stepped back to the microphones. "His name is his Excellency Samuel Harbinger, Bishop of the village of Lipoppo in Kenya. He has chosen to be known as Pope Samuel I."

The crowd erupted with joy.

The new pope walked out into the bright sunshine and waved to the crowd massed below him. In a festive, almost playful mood, well-wishers and visitors from all parts of the world cheered and greeted him with a sea of Vatican flags and white handkerchiefs. The pope laughed when a group of schoolchildren began throwing their caps in the air.

The pontiff whispered to Cardinal Vortel. "Is there a stool or a wooden box that I can stand on? The people can hardly see me."

"Holiness, just keep waving to the crowd. I'll find you something."

Minutes later, an out of breath Cardinal Vortel returned carrying a small ladder. "There was not an empty box to be found. This will have to do."

The pontiff balanced himself on the ladder. "It's fine."

* * * * * *

When the chanting began to subside, Pope Samuel turned to Cardinal Vortel.

"What now, Your Eminence?"

"Give them your blessing—*Urbi et Orbi.*"

"What's that mean?"

"In Latin, it means to the City of Rome and to the World."

"Can I give my blessing in English?"

Vortel consulted with the secretary of state.

"Better in Latin, Your Holiness. If you give it in English, you'll upset the French and the Russians. Welcome to the world of Vatican politics."

"Then what about using Swahili?"

"You'll probably offend the Italians, and God knows, maybe even the Americans. Using Latin offends no one. It is still the official language of the church."

"I'll need some coaching to give it in Latin."

Vortel scribbled some Latin words on a scrap of paper.

"Here, Your Holiness, just read this."

"Your Eminence, I can't read your handwriting."

Cardinal Vortel winced. "Then we have no choice—do the best you can with the Latin, Holiness. I'll stand next to you if you forget the words."

Pope Samuel cleared his throat. "*In Nominen Partis.*"

Two mistakes in three words—it could be worse, Vortel thought.

"*Et Filiae.*"

The camerlengo blanched. He was sure he had heard it right. The new pope had just blessed the world in the name of the Father and of the Daughter, (*Filia*), not in the name of the Father and of the Son, (*Filius*). Luckily, at that moment the loud speakers malfunctioned, drowning out the last syllable of the word.

"*Et Sanctus Spiritutem.*"

Vortel didn't know where to begin correcting Pope Samuel's reference to the Holy Ghost. But if the Holy Ghost wanted this man to be Pope, Vortel was sure that the matter would be resolved between them.

When the pontiff had ended his blessing, the crowd started clapping their hands spontaneously.

Vortel whispered in Pope Samuel's ear. "Preach to the crowd before they start to drift away, Your Holiness."

For a moment, Pope Samuel stood paralyzed. He knew that all eyes were on him. By this time, word of his election had spread among his friends in Lipoppo. Obani would have seen to that. In fact by now, the whole village would most likely be sitting in front of the rectory, watching his first blessing on Zamba's old television set. By now, word of his election would most likely have spread to

Christina Hagerbloom in Oslo, to John Wedgwood and Francis Baellert in Boston, to Secretary General Theocritus in New York, and to Tomas Brandzek in Schenectady. He wondered whether his friends Bartholomew, Tad, and Mary had heard. He hoped they were not giving up on the idea of running guided tours of old New York neighborhoods.

Pope Samuel pulled the microphones closer.

"I live in Africa in a small village that lies on the outskirts of a savannah."

The crowd grew silent as the pontiff began to speak. Miraculously, he did not stutter.

"One day as I passed the water hole in my village of Lipoppo, I noticed a curious thing. There was a long line of wildebeest, maybe thirty in number, with their heads down drinking the water. One wildebeest, however, kept his head up and did not drink. It was obvious that his job was to warn the rest of the herd of any impending danger. Then I noticed that other wildebeests were not drinking as well. Some patrolled the borders of the herd to keep calves from wandering off. Others kept watch over pregnant cows to help them when they went into labor. The herd had created a network of guardians and caretakers whose responsibility it was to protect members of the herd at their most vulnerable moments.

"All of us here today are protected by our own guardians. In my church, we call these guardians 'angels.' They do not wear long, white robes; they do not have wings or carry trumpets. No, angels are quite ordinary looking. They look like you and me. Why is that so, you might ask? It is because they *are* you and I. We are angels to others and others are angels to us.

"Let me leave you now. It has been a full day for me. It is not often that you are elected Pope. But before I go, let me bow to all of you—you are my angels. I pray that as my co-popes, you will help me carry out the mission God has asked of me."

The pope finished speaking to the crowd in St. Peter's Square, left the balcony, and stepped back inside the basilica.

With a look of relief on his face, Pope Samuel turned to Cardinal Vortel.

"How did I do, Your Eminence?"

"Your homily was wonderful, but we have to do a little work on your Latin vocabulary—particularly the difference between *filius* and *filia*."

"Did I mix up the names again? *Filius* is 'girl,' isn't it?"

"No, Holiness, it's the other way around. *Filius* means 'son' and *filia* means 'daughter.'"

"So I blessed the world in the name of …"

"Yes, Holiness, you blessed the world in the name of God the father's daughter."

* * * * * *

That night Pope Samuel called Lipoppo. The phone was busy. He wondered if Zamba's wife would ever finish talking. On the fourth attempt, the Holy Father finally got through to his housekeeper.

When Bagua heard Samuel's voice, she began to cry.

"Why are you crying, Bagua?"

"Bishop Samuel, if you must live in Rome, who will wash and iron your clothes?"

"There are those who do these things here in Rome."

"And what about your favorite foods—who will know how to cook hippo stew?"

"Bagua, you know I'm a vegetarian. I don't eat hippo stew."

"Well, then who will know how to cook your favorite bean stew?"

"Cook it yourself. Come to Rome and be my housekeeper, Bagua."

"I don't know where Rome is or how to get there. Is it near Nairobi? I was there once."

"No, but Nelson will help you get here. I will ask him to buy you airline tickets."

227

"Must I go to Rome on a plane? I will be afraid when the plane leaves the ground and goes high in the sky."

"Say a prayer to God—he will protect you from harm."

"And what about my family?"

"In Rome, there are jobs for your husband and schools for your children."

"If these things are so, then I will come to Rome and be your housekeeper."

"Good."

"But what about Banda, Samuel?"

The pope held back his tears. "Mobeki has gone to speak to him."

* * * * * *

That night drums sounded all over Africa as the people danced for joy at the election of one of their sons as the Vicar of Jesus Christ.

That night, the lion Banda also listened to the sound of the drums. They brought sadness to his heart, however.. Mobeki had come to tell him that Samuel was now the pope..

"A pope must live in Rome, Banda. But Samuel promises that he will come to visit you and the others as soon as he can. In the meantime, he hopes you are staying east of the line of acacia trees."

When Mobeki left, Banda began to whimper. He loved his friend Samuel so much. He wondered if there was some way he could travel to Rome and pay his friend a surprise visit. He wondered how far Rome was from Lipoppo. Maybe one of the animals at the water hole would know, he thought.

The drums slowly quieted, but Banda continued to sit near the stand of acacia trees late into the night.

Cast of Characters

(If you find yourself in these pages, you have made a terrible mistake! Any similarity to actual individuals is purely coincidental.)

The Village of Lipoppo

Agatha – the village dressmaker who asks the tough questions

Father Albert – pastor of the parish of Woomba who struggles with his vocation as a priest

Bagua – Father Harbinger's housekeeper who cooks hippo stew for her vegetarian boss

Banda – a male lion that lives near the water hole and is a friend of Father Harbinger. Banda is easily corrupted by a candy bar

Samuel Harbinger – Bishop of Lipoppo and protagonist of the story

Hestern – village carpenter and mortal enemy of women who might try to pursue Bishop Harbinger

Kareri – village seamstress who takes her time in making a child's confirmation outfit

Lacata – resident of Woomba who has lost a husband and a son

Mark and Martha – students who were chosen by the Council of Elders of Lipoppo to study at Harvard University

Miriam – an elderly woman who helps in the AIDS clinic and who knows that kingombo is okra

Mobeki – village mechanic and close friend of Father Harbinger.

Nelson – village banker who convinces Father Harbinger of the need for tagging black pieces of luggage with pictures or colored ribbons

Ningoro – village cobbler and father of Mark

Obani – village postman who is always ready to help his parish priest

Slocum – bush pilot in Kenya who is the first to land an airplane in Lipoppo

Theresa Undala – a child who dies of AIDS

Village children – serve the pope's Mass

Yobate – Father Albert's housekeeper who is wary of Lacata

Zamba – village blacksmith who, like Hestern, is an enemy of designing women

Zamba's wife – constantly on the telephone to learn about her grandchild

New York City

Becu – security officer at the United Nations

Seth Benjamin – protocol officer who works in the New York City Mayor's Office

Monsignor "Spooky" Crenshaw – protocol officer who works for the New York Archdiocese

Early Morning Jogger – joins march up Fifth Avenue as far as Starbucks

Governor of New York – decides not to come to the Harbinger gala

Julia Harbinger – Vincent Harbinger's wife and a snazzy dresser

Vincent Harbinger – older brother of Samuel Harbinger and owner of the Harlem night club named The Conclave

Kevin Larkin – deputy inspector of the New York City Police Department, and a man of solutions

Mary Madeline – a prostitute who changes her occupation

The Mayor – the chief elected official of the City of New York, experiences the joys of protocol

Bartholomew McDermott – worker who searches for the perfect chocolate egg cream

Police Sergeant – helps on the walk to the Bronx Zoo

Thaddeus – taxicab driver and close friend of Bartholomew McDermott

Basil Theocritus – Cypriot-born Secretary General of the United Nations who learns the value of okra

Harvard University

Francis Baellert – Dean of the Harvard Graduate School who learns how to ride a bicycle despite his fear of bruised knees

Sean Baellert – son of Francis Baellert who befriends students from Lipoppo, and introduces Mark and Martha to the McDonald's fast food chain

Felice Fergusine – Harvard University's counselor for African students who advocates a very liberal, liberal arts curriculum

Professor of Classics – an academic cross-dresser with a love of Latin aphorisms

Roland Polycarp Sekkoes – a trafficker in drugs and a would-be philanthropist

John Wedgewood – President of Harvard University

The Vatican

Pope Linus II – Vicar of Christ, Servant of the Servants of God, Pontiff of the Catholic Church, Bishop of Rome, and owner of a corgi puppy. No one denies he has his hands full.

Cardinals – electors of the pope; they wear red to distinguish themselves from everybody else in the world. Once a cardinal turns eighty, he loses his right to vote for a new pope but continues to cause trouble from the sidelines.

Sebastiano Bagonninni – Vatican Secretary of State and number two man in the government of the Holy See. His name is probably too long by two n's.

Ugo Carpaccio – Dean of the College of Cardinals; age has engendered respect

Martin Jensen – Prefect of the Congregation for Bishops; the betting man's choice to be the next pope

Tung Bin Kim – still not an octogenarian in his own mind

Richard Plimpton – Archbishop of New York; the betting man's choice to be the pope if Martin Jensen does not have the votes

Josef Vortel – Camerlengo of the Catholic Church; the official appointed to administer the church during the period between the death of one pope and the election of his successor.

Bishops – successors of Saint Peter, they are branch managers of the church, running the more than three thousand dioceses in the world. Archbishops are bishops promoted to govern bigger dioceses and are most likely on their way to becoming a cardinal.

Virgilio Patti – the Papal Master of Liturgical Ceremonies; keeps candidates in line

Monsignors - Monsignor is a rank between a bishop and a priest.

Paolo Remigi – the pope's personal secretary, and often heralded as a future Pope

Priests

Assistant to Cardinal Bagonninni – a repository of malicious gossip

Ignatius Cropsy – a friend of Samuel Harbinger with a dislike of airplane takeoffs and landings

Andre Mabibin – assistant to Cardinal Jensen, who is allegedly able to find heresy in the *Pater Noster*

John Palestro – Dominican monk and friend of Ignatius Cropsy

Rector of the Gregorian University – a Jesuit. Need I say more.

Sisters

Sister Consuela – Pope Linus' housekeeper and overseer of his pills

Other characters in the novel

Andrew Ableworthy – President of the United States

Argentine Minister to the United Nations – has genuine feelings for the UN Secretary General

Sergio Bonti – a reporter for the Rome daily *Il Messaggero*; sees a good story in Samuel Harbinger's ordination as a bishop

Tomas Brandzek – a student from Schenectady, New York

Giuseppe Chimati – proprietor of Dignitas, a print shop for clerical business cards

Gilbert Cleverhand – United States Secretary of State

Commandant of the Swiss Guards – head of the quaintly dressed Vatican police force

Jacob Dayer – Foreign Minister of Israel; the reality of the rogue is not lost on him

Cesare Duo – Director of the Vatican's Telecommunications Department

Giovanni – a twenty-year-old, employed at the switchboard in the *Domus Sanctae Marthae*

Holy Spirit – third person of the Blessed Trinity also named the Holy Ghost and the Paraclete. It is said the Holy Spirit leads the College of Cardinals to the next pope.

Signor Manelli – head Vatican tailor who does some of his best work in the backseats of cars

Mahmood Mylas – Foreign Minister of the Palestine Liberation Organization. He is not afraid to risk his life for a priest

Prefect of the Papal Household – a Vatican factotum

The Queen of England – donor of a corgi to Pope Linus, otherwise ruler of Great Britain

Duke Rayner – Middle East correspondent for *The New York Times*. In the end, he gives Bishop Harbinger a chance

Security Official at Rome Airport – starts Harbinger on his search for his bicycle

Vatican Technician – keeps the Sistine Chapel free of listening devices

Doctor Marcello Tussi – Pope Linus' medical doctor

Waiter at *Domus Sanctae Marthae* – critic of Cardinal Jensen

Oslo

King Haakon V and Queen Charlotte of Norway – the perfect model of a modern day royal family

Christina Hagerbloom – member of the Nobel Peace Prize Committee, and happy to pay for lunch

Chants and Sings

"Litany of the Saints" – a request of saints to intercede in the affairs of men, and is usually chanted in Latin

Tu es Petrus – "You Are Peter" – papal national anthem

Veni Creator Spiritus – a request to the Holy Spirit to inspire the Catholic Church to follow along the proper path

"When the Saints Go Marching In" – a New Orleans spiritual

The Animals

Police dogs

Gabriel's elephants

Fides – the pope's corgi

A leopard

A lioness – one who pursues Harbinger

A rouge elephant

A zebra named Serena

Inanimate Objects

Bicycle

Stools, ladders, and telephone directories

Hippo stew – Yummy!

Gerald T. McLaughlin lives in Pacific Palisades, California. An authority on commercial law, McLaughlin has taught at Fordham, Georgetown, Brooklyn, and the University of Connecticut law schools. From 1991 to 2000, he served as Dean of Loyola Law School in Los Angeles. In 2005, McLaughlin published his first novel entitled The Parchment.

LaVergne, TN USA
13 November 2009
163956LV00003B/17/P